Money for noth

and my T

Richard Murphy

The Finance Press

Money for nothing and my Tweets for free
Richard Murphy

◆

First published by The Finance Press 2022

ISBN 978-1-8384731-1-2

Cover design and layout by
David Mullins of dambrilliant.com
cover image adapted from shutterstock.com

Tax Research LLP
33 Kingsley Walk, Ely, CB6 3BZ, United Kingdom
http://www.taxresearch.org.uk/Blog/

Donations to support the work of Tax Research UK can be made at http://www.taxresearch.org.uk/Blog/

Contents

Foreword

When I began writing long Twitter threads to explain some of my economic thinking late in 2020 there was no plan underpinning that process. It was only because the first one seemed to be popular that I wrote another. And then a third. And so it continued.

Logically those Tweets should not have worked. It was a little odd to think of creating an argument in up to eighty paragraphs of no more than 280 characters. It was even stranger to imagine that people might then read the resulting Twitter threads, often without unrolling them.

But they did. One thread has reached more than 1.5 million people and has had more than 125,000 interactions, so far. The least I could assume as a consequence was that something resonated.

I reposted the threads on my blog[1]. There they created less of a reaction. Maybe that's because what I had to say was familiar to many of my regular readers on that site. However, requests for the threads to be republished as PDFs happened, quite often. Those were made with regard to individual threads. But then it occurred to me that if I was going to do one thread I might as well assemble the threads into an ebook and put them out together.

'Money for nothing and my Tweets for free' is the result.

1 Tax Research UK http://www.taxresearch.org.uk/Blog/

All the chapters in this ebook began life as Twitter threads, barring two. Those exceptions are my fantasy radio interview (chapter 9) and that on funding the Green New Deal (chapter 4). Both seemed to fit the theme of the rest of the ebook and they were written during the same four month period in which the threads were published and so I made exceptions in their cases. Both began life as a blog posts.

It's also fair to note that all but one of the threads were written without this book in mind. The exception is the one on inflation. That, I admit, was written to fill a gap, as well as to address a real issue.

What is consistent is that every chapter, however it originated, was written quickly, and often in a single sitting of no more than three hours. A persistent and relentless energy should, therefore, be apparent in them. That relentlessness was motivated by the desire to explain what I saw as a critical issue when I wrote them[2].

I do think economics is critical. It shapes the way that we live our lives. Too few people, in my opinion, understand just how the assumptions of economists, most of them working in academic ivory towers in which they appear more remote from reality than most in the academic world, shape the possibilities with which we are presented, let alone the choices we actually make.

It is the consequence of the assumptions that a majority of economists have made that government is seen as inefficient and that markets are almost always to be

2 In many cases it was also, to be candid, driven by the desire to stop writing and have breakfast.

preferred when any need is to be met. Likewise, it is the assumptions of some economists that suggested that austerity should dominate the politics of the last decade.

It was also economists who suggested that the 2008 crisis was not a sign of the structural failure of the model that they themselves had created, which meant it survived that catastrophic failure unreformed, leaving us ill-prepared for Covid.

As a graduate economist, who became a chartered accountant, entrepreneur, tax specialist in a practicing firm, and then a campaigner for tax and economic justice before going on to join academia, I like to think I see the world a little differently from most economists. It's not that I don't make assumptions, because we all do all the time. It is that I hope that my thinking is a little more rooted in reality than that of the average economist is.

That is not to knock economics. I like economic theory. I read it. If I have to, I can do some of the maths that goes with a lot of it. But the truth is that even those who try to pigeonhole me into a theory don't really get the fact that my over-arching principle is that pragmatism has to prevail.

So, for example, those who know modern monetary theory (MMT) will see that it influences much of what is in the ebook, at least with regard to money and its relationship to government and government spending. I happen to think that MMT gets much of that right.

However, much as I like what MMT has done in that area, I think it has blinded itself on tax and on the role of tax in society, which it underplays. In addition, on savings and its relationship to both money creation and inequality I am not sure that MMT has yet to even notice that there is an issue for it to address, but I have. In that case the MMT purist might find issues that irritate them in this ebook. I am unapologetic for that. Irritation is the cause of most progress.

My approach is, then, to look at the real world first, and to use the insights that theory provides to mould what I believe are pragmatic answers that can exist within the real constraints that society imposes (rightly or wrongly) to provide workable solutions to the actual problems that we face. If that tramples on any theoreticians' toes, so be it.

This conflict with pure theory is almost inevitable, anyway. That is because what I do is applied political economy, and not economic theory. In applied political economy, unlike economics, there is no assumption that there is an ideal form of economy. Market fundamentalists and hardcore socialists will, in that case, be disappointed by my approach. I believe in the private sector, whilst recognising that it is riddled with faults. I also think government is a fantastic tool for delivering many of the things that we need. It just so happens it can also fail to do that. I can live with the paradoxes and inconsistencies. Day-to-day we all do.

What that means is that instead of looking for perfect theoretical worlds, in applied political economy the question is, very often, why do we fail? The answer invariably comes down to the fact that we're human. We're not good at a number of really important things. Complexity is one of them. Pragmatism is another. Compromise is a third. Managing uncertainty is a fourth. We also suffer a number of self-limiting traits. Vanity, greed and belief in our own importance rank high amongst these, and I will acknowledge straightaway that I have been accused of all three before anyone does so for me. These things are the given truths of applied political economy for me. They mean that things will go wrong.

And the distribution of income and wealth and so power in society, which is a given in society at any point in time, has the marked propensity to make things worse, meaning it too is a significant factor to take into account in applied political economy.

My point in saying this is to suggest that economic theory is not always a great tool, by itself, to suggest a way out of the resulting mess. That mess is too complex in its nature and its extent to be captured within any one theory. Nor is any theory necessarily very enduring, because the reality is that the mess we humans create appears to be endlessly capable of adaptation. The emergence of the climate crisis is evidence of that, and changes pretty much every assumption we have made to date.

What I am suggesting, in that case, is that there is no perfect solution to an economics problem. I would have thought we should have learned that by now, but apparently not. Instead economics, on both the left and right, still pursues the idea that there is some 'ideal state' to which we are headed, whether it is the pure market economy or socialism, or some other 'ideal'. That though, is not true. Not only does no such ideal exist, as indicated by the fact that all of them have their opponents, but nor are they possible. And the idea that these mythical ideals represent some sort of economic nirvana is in any case just wrong: the propensity for human error will be just as strong in an ideal state as it is now, and without the moderating common sense that is essential if an economy is to work. That is why I look for practical answers to current questions, rather than seek to promote a theory. What I seek to do is mix an understanding of theory with a dose of experience to which I add a portion of ethics to suggest solutions.

The ethics in question are, I admit, pretty important. Remember too that there is nothing unusual in this. When Adam Smith published what is considered to be the first book on economics in 1776[3] it was thought to be a work of moral philosophy. Many, in fact, saw it as a footnote to his previous work, entitled 'The Theory of Moral Sentiments'[4]. Ethics and economics do mix, but not quite as explicitly these days as I think they should.

In my case the ethics I use are pretty simple, but powerful. It is my belief that if any society is to survive it must expect that each person should be treated as well as we expect to be treated, and that this is a rule that applies both collectively and individually. As is typical of my own more theoretical work, what this does is to reduce the guidance for behaviour to the minimum number

3 The Wealth of Nations, which is still in print
4 Also still in print

of variables possible. You and I are of equal worth, and should treat each other as such, is what I am saying, and I am also saying that this will hold true whoever you and I might be. The logic is one of reciprocal wellbeing. That explains what motivates the thinking in this ebook. That the idea happens to be embraced by every major wisdom and religious tradition of which I am aware just helps.

In practice the book is split into ten chapters. All were written between mid-November 2020 and mid-March 2021[5]. I have written a relatively brief introduction to each chapter, giving a very little background information and to them and then I let the thread or blog post speak for itself.

I have resisted the temptation to edit the threads, three very minor exceptions apart, all of which have been used very sparingly. First spelling and punctuation errors have been corrected. Second, in one case a minor factual error has been corrected. And third, if a Tweet appeared confusing I have sought to add clarity, but that has only been done very occasionally. Otherwise I have left what I originally wrote alone, deciding that if it worked in the first instance then it should also do so now.

There is inevitable duplication, repetition and overlap between the threads, and so chapters, as a result. I could, I suppose, have edited that out. The result would, however, have been a very different. And, anyway, I saw no merit in doing so. Nothing I think that I say here is very complicated. But, that said, many have described at least some of it as mind blowing because it challenges

5 To put this in context, I wrote about 400 blog posts during this period: this ebook reflects a small part of my output. For the rest go to http://www.taxresearch.org.uk/Blog/

what we have long been told to be true. When rethinking long held assumptions the repetition of new ideas, in slightly different forms, can be necessary, so I make no apology for doing so.

The structuring of the chapters does not follow the order in which they were first published. That is largely because there was no book in mind when I wrote them, so they were not required to have a logical flow. Subject to the caveat that each thread went where I felt it was necessary to go to make the overall argument that I am seeking to present, I have structured them as follows.

Chapter one is an introduction to my overall theme. This chapter spends time considering the nature of money, how it is created and what it represents within the overall theme of managing the economy, which is the dominant issue that these combined chapters seeks to address. Because money is so widely misunderstood, including by most economists, getting this basic understanding right is essential. For that reason the theme reappears again in several other chapters, and most especially in chapter 6, which was the most successful thread that now appears in this ebook. In that case if you don't get chapter 1 on first reading try chapter 6 next, even if it says it is on the theme of debt because it is also about some economic fundamentals.

In chapter 2 I discuss the phenomena of quantitative easing, or QE as it is now called, which has changed so much about what we understand about government financing in the last decade or so, to the extent that nothing now is remotely like it was in this field in 2007. The fact is that now, unlike then, we know government can create money at will, and this changes everything. I elaborate this theme in Chapter 3, where the link between QE and funding the Green New Deal is explored.

That in turn leads to a more detailed discussion in chapter 4 on how to fund the investment that we need to transform our society and make it sustainable. I make no apology for labouring this point so early in the book. The most common question asked by journalists and others of politicians who say that they want to transform society is 'How are you going to pay for it?' I wanted to make clear, upfront, that I can answer this question: money is not a problem or an obstacle to creating the world that I think we both want and need.

In chapters 5 and 6 I address the issue of debt. The so-called national debt is fuelling a national political paranoia that is crippling our society so the issue is worth two chapters. My argument is that we needn't worry about this issue. I unashamedly offer two takes on this theme. It was important enough to require two threads. Both get a place in here.

After that I turn in chapter 7 to one of my own favourite themes, which is tax. As with money and debt, I argue that we misunderstand the role of tax in our society. Even those on the left who profess their belief in tax usually make the mistake of thinking that tax pays for government spending. By the time that you reach Chapter 7 in this book I sincerely hope that this misconception should have been put firmly in its place. Tax does not pay for any government spending. What it does instead do is reclaim the money that the government spends into the economy to make sure that inflation is under control. In this context it plays an incredibly significant role in the management of the economy. That does not mean it pays for anything, but what that role does also mean is that tax is also a powerful instrument for the delivery of social and economic policy. It is these issues that are discussed in chapter 7.

Having mentioned inflation, the whole of chapter 8 is dedicated to that issue. In particular, I suggest why I think inflation is unlikely in the UK at present, and why those promoting the idea that it might be really have other social agendas in play that should be ignored, as the Biden administration appears to be doing in the USA.

Finally, in chapters 9 and 10 I turn to the application of some ideas. In chapter 9 the application is in the form of a fantasy radio interview, where an informed person answers the usual nonsense asked by interviewers on programmes like 'Today' on BBC Radio 4. I have been on that programme, but not of late, and not on these issues. The BBC and other broadcasters are deeply reluctant to consider the possibility that there are alternative economic narratives to the one driven by debt paranoia that they insist on presenting to the nation. It would be great to change this.

Chapter 10, finally, looks at the power relationships in play in a real issue that is likely to rumble on for a while. This is the nurses' pay dispute. As I explain, there is much more to this than the simple issue of 'affordability' that the government claims to be the case. The government's ability to afford what they want has now been exposed. There are, then, power politics at play here. The real question is who does the government want to benefit from the way that they run the economy? It would seem clear that it is not NHS nurses. The chapter looks at the consequences.

In the process it suggests how I look at applied political economy. Everything in that subject is about the use of power to reward some, and potentially prejudice others. The question it asks is for whose benefit do we structure society? The answers that this government provides are unappealing. And that is what motivate me to write these threads. There will, no doubt, be more to come.

Richard Murphy

Ely, Cambridgeshire
March 2021

◆

1. Economics

This thread was posted by me on Twitter on 12 December 2020[1]. It wasn't the first thread that I posted that appears in this book, but it was the first where I tried to pull my economics ideas together. More than 1.25 million people have been reached by this thread and over 70,000 people have engaged with it.

The type of economics that I address in this thread and chapter is what is described as macroeconomics. This is that part of economics that deals with the economies of countries and governments. It also addresses issues such as government income and spending, and so tax, as well as the national debt, the role of central banks, inflation and the balance of trade.

It is an aspect of economics that, despite its importance, engages only a very small part of the economics profession. The vast majority of economists deal with microeconomics. That part of economics deals with the behaviour of individuals, companies and markets.

Economists like microeconomics because it can be used to construct deeply theoretical, largely mathematical, models of behaviour that, if truth be told, tell us very little at all about how real people, companies or markets behave. That is because of the simplifying assumptions that too many economists use in the course of their work.

1 https://twitter.com/RichardJMurphy/status/1337737606688333826

Those assumptions assure them of two things. The first is that their maths works, which is of greatest significance to them. Second, it guarantees that they produce outcomes that show markets are invariably more efficient than governments, which is something far too many economists set out to prove in their own particular way.

I am not saying microeconomics is not important. I think it is, but not in the way that many economists do it. I just happen to think macroeconomics is more important. And I discuss it as a matter of preference because far too much of what is said about macroeconomics is quite explicitly based on microeconomic thinking that, as a result, reproduces the result that microeconomics is set up to deliver, which is that government is not as efficient as markets.

I approach the subject differently. I look at the real world. I try to make as few assumptions as possible. Because I am also a qualified accountant I also tend to follow the cash - which few economists do. And I look for real world solutions to problems, and not ideal outcomes that will never exist in practice. The result is a very different approach to economics.

Of course, I am not alone in doing this. There are others of similar persuasion, I am pleased to say. But my crossover between accountancy and economics is very rare. And I think that produces a different view on the economy based on having in my time managed real activity, which I did for many years. This chapter is the result of that approach.

As the best waiter might say, 'Enjoy'.

◆

I keep hearing people complain that the 'mainstream media' does not understand economics and that we're talked down to as if everything must be explained as if the economy is a household. In this thread I explain all you (and they) need to know. Economics in one thread then...

Very few people seem to understand how money is created. Mainly that's because when they're told it seems so simple that they can't believe something that's so important that we're willing to pay a lot to get it is created so easily. This thread explains how money is created.

What this thread also explains is that if we understand money we can completely reimagine how the economy really works, which is the pathway to rebuilding from the mess we are in. That makes this a pretty big deal. I make no apology for its length as a result.

Let's start at the very beginning. A person goes into a bank and asks for a £1,000 loan. The bank checks them out, and agrees. And that is all that it takes to create new money. Money is just a promise to pay. That simple exchange of promises is all it takes to create it.

Most people think there must be something that backs up the value of money. Gold, most likely. But there isn't. Money is just a promise to pay, and has been for almost 50 years now. Mutual promises to pay creates all the money we have.

So in the example of that £1,000 loan, the customer promises to pay the bank. So the bank opens a loan account for them. That records their promise to repay. And the bank puts £1,000 in the customer's current account. They promise to let the customer spend that how they want.

Two promises. Two accounts. And as a result we get new money. That is how all money is created. It is as simple as that.

There is no one else's money involved in this process. The bank does not lend out the money saved with them. And there are no notes and coin moved from one pile to another pile to back this all up either. There are just two promises. And then there is new money.

Making money really is as simple as promising to repay it. So why is it so expensive for some people to get hold of it? That's not because the money itself is expensive. Clearly, it isn't. That's because there's a risk that they will break their promise.

Money itself is really cheap. The pure price of borrowing money has been falling for hundreds of years. It is now officially 0.1% per annum in the UK. That's the rate set by the Bank of England. Or just £1 a year for every £1,000 borrowed. Which is staggeringly cheap.

That's the rate the government pays. Around £800 billion of money deposited by UK banks and building societies with the Bank of England gets interest paid on it at 0.1% a year. And if the Bank decided the rate could be 0%, or even negative.

So the reality is that money is almost free. In fact, allowing for inflation, which is higher than this interest rate, money is free to the government. In reality people are paying the government to hold their money.

But the government borrows more cheaply than anyone else. It creates the currency - the pound - and declares it legal tender. And it has its own bank - the Bank of England. This means the government can lend to itself. So it can never run out of money. It is risk free.

The rest of us don't have a bank, and can't declare the money we make to be legal tender. So, all other lending is riskier. Including the money that you lend to your bank, which is exactly what you are doing if you have a bank account that's in credit.

If you think you have 'money in the bank', think again. You have not. You just have a promise from the bank to pay you money if you demand it. And if they can pay it, of course. You're now the banker. They're the borrower. And you have the risk they won't repay.

And that risk is real. Remember Northern Rock? The government stepped in. This is why all bank deposits in the UK have to be guaranteed by the government to a limit of £85,000. If they weren't it's likely no one would trust the banks to repay.

But what this means is that for most people (not the wealthiest, and not big business) the government guarantees all the money that we have. And it even, by implication, guarantees that the banks exist so that they are there to lend if and when we require it.

How is it possible that although all money is made by promises - including yours, and mine - the government is so important? First, it alone creates the currency. Secondly, as I noted, it has its own bank. So it can always repay, because it will always lend it money.

So, it's the government and it's the Bank of England, and their promise to pay that is actually behind the real value of our money. Not gold. Not notes. Not coins. Not how strong the rest of the UK banking system is. The promise that the government makes is what matters.

But why is its promise so good? Because it has the means to back it up. Having a bank is not enough. Having the means to tax changes everything. That, and the ability to pass law to make sure tax is paid. And then only in the currency the government chooses - the pound.

Tax is what gives the pound its value. If the government could just create money without limit it would soon be worthless. But it does not do that. Tax ensures that the government can control the amount of money in the economy.

A lot of that money is created by the government. Every time it spends it tells the Bank of England to pay whoever is required. And it does that, because it trusts the promise the government makes to repay it. Well, it would, wouldn't it? After all, the government owns it.
But what the Bank of England does not do is check

whether it's got money available to lend the government to spend. It does not need to do so, after all. All it need do is trust the government's promise to repay. And then it creates the money that the government wants to spend.

This is really important though. What it means is that tax does not need to be collected before the government spends. Instead, the government always spends the money its bank creates for it when instructed to do so.

But that means something else. It means the government never spends taxpayers' money.

It also means that tax does not fund spending. That can happen without tax.

So what does tax do? It does something really important. It recovers the money the government has spent into the economy. Enough has to be collected to control inflation and make good on the promise that the government gives when it guarantees all our money.

Does that mean the government has to balance its books? No way does it mean that. Controlling inflation is the goal, and what we've learned is we can run deficits, and control inflation.

But that has come at a big price to date. That price has been unemployment, low wages and lots of crap jobs that add little value to society or the lives of those who do them. To be polite, that's the economic policy of a callous government that does not care.

Forcing people into meaningless, low paid work is a price too high to control inflation, even if that also means lower taxes and that deficits do not threaten to create economic instability. There has to be a better way to manage the value of money than this.

And there is. We could have a government promise full employment. It could create the jobs we need. It could force up the minimum wage by guaranteeing local work for anyone who wanted it. And we could improve benefits too. All using government made money. Not tax.

But would there be inflation then? Not if we then taxed enough and cut spending a bit. But people at work in good jobs do pay more tax. And they claim fewer benefits. So that condition is easy to meet. And if we still needed more tax? Well, we could do that, if needed.

But that need would not be to fund the spend. Tax is never needed to fund spending. Always remember that. It's needed to control inflation. And to redistribute income and wealth, and other social reasons. But not to fund spending. Ever. Money does that.

So, I hear you say, why do governments borrow then? After all, if they can create all the money that they need why do they have to borrow other people's money? Doesn't the fact that they borrow prove me wrong? No, it doesn't. Because they don't need to borrow.

The government did have to borrow when money was in short supply. That was when it was backed by gold. That system ended way back in the last century[2]. Since then, remember, all money is just a promise to pay. But also remember, the government has by far the best promise.

So, people who are cautious, like big pension funds, large companies, the wealthy and banks themselves want somewhere as safe to save as ordinary people - those with less than £85,000 in their bank account - have right now. And that means they want to save with the government.

But they cannot in ordinary bank accounts because the government has set a limit on the amount that can be saved in them. So the government has adapted a gold standard era savings mechanism to meet this need for a safe savings account in the modern world of money.

That mechanism is 'the gilt'. Gilt, of course, is gold. Once the certificates for these were printed with a gold edge. Not any more they are not, of course. Remember, everything about money is just a promise to pay now. Gilts, or government bonds, are like everything else in this regard.

And money is not scarce for the government now, either. It could have all it needs on overdraft at the Bank of England if it wanted. And it need not pay interest on that. So why doesn't it go for this cheapest of all funding options? Because people need safety, that's why not.

So, just as the government guarantees most people's money in the bank, it also offers gilts (or government bonds) for those with millions or billions to save because they too want guarantees on their money. And they will accept a low rate of interest to get it.

Government bonds are not, then, real borrowing by the government. They are instead a savings mechanism. Sure, they look like a loan. But then so too is a building society bond a loan to a building society. But it's also a savings account in reality.

And that's what government bonds are: they are just savings accounts. That's all. And, as I noted above when I explained how money is created, savers' money is not involved in money creation by lending, at all.

In the same way, government borrowing is not in involved in the funding of its spending. Sure, the government borrows. But then all savings institutions do, all the time. But they don't lend savers' money out. And the government doesn't fund spending with borrowing either.

And before questions are asked about quantitative easing (QE) and where this fits in, let me address that one[2]. QE is a process that involves the government buying back gilts. So, it is a mechanism to control the amount of savings it makes available. That's it. No more.

QE also controls the amount of money in the banking system. QE forces money out of government gilts because the government buys them back, making them scarcer. The flip side is that government pays for these bonds using free money that the Bank of England creates for it.

2 Also see the next chapter

This money creation puts more money into commercial banks, backing up the government guarantee that they will be solvent. That money injection is pretty important in that case.

But just to add to the list of what QE does, it also shatters the myth that governments are under the thumb of bond markets, for good. Now if bond markets get uppity about anything the government simply has the power to buy its debt back and bond dealers are left high and dry.

And another QE fact; by controlling the money supply into commercial banks the government gains almost complete control of short-term interest rates, and through QE it has a massive influence on long term rates too. QE delivers protection from economic shocks as a result.

I'm not saying QE is a universal good, by the way. It's forced money into the stock market and overinflated it. That has increased inequality. Neither is good news. But it does add a powerful weapon to the government armoury for controlling the economy.

So, the government can now create money at will, control how much of that is in commercial banks and in government backed savings accounts at any time, control inflation through the tax system and deliver full employment if it wants, all if we understand money. Pretty cool, then.

But to make sure this is clear, where does this new knowledge that comes from the very simple understanding of how money is created (not printed, or made - created is the right word) leave us?

First, it says the government underpins the value of all our money, because whilst all money is a promise to pay, the government's promise is the best, and our banks could not function without the support of that promise. We need to remind arrogant bankers of that, often.

Second, whilst cash saving is important to people it's also pretty important to realise that it is much like dead money. It is not used to fund bank lending or to pay for government spending. That does really mean the state should not be subsidising it with things like ISAs.

Third, spend comes before tax, always.

Fourth, the government always spends its money, and not taxpayers'.

Fifth, tax does not fund government spending. Tax is instead used to control inflation, redistribute income and reorganise the economy, but never to fund spending, and that's true in any country with its own central bank and currency and that never use another country's currency.

Sixth, the government does not need to borrow because it can always create the money it needs on overdraft at the Bank of England.

Seventh, the borrowing it does do is a favour to those who want to save with the government. It does never need the money people save with it.

Eighth, that means we need never have a debt crisis. If we don't need people's money, because the government can always create its own, where's the debt crisis? Especially when a government can always repay on demand, simply by asking the Bank of England to make the payment?

Ninth, the amount of savings a government wants to accept, and the interest rate it now has to pay on it, can always now be controlled through the QE system. All this does is regulate the government backed, cash based, savings system. Nothing more, and nothing less.

Tenth, I stress, that means all interest rates are now heavily influenced by the government and many are under its direct control. So where is the interest rate panic?

Eleventh, inflation is not now controlled by interest rates - because we don't want them to rise. It's going to be controlled by tax. I admit, right now no one has an ideal tax to achieve this goal. I am working on it. It is possible. And it's progressive, and so fair.

Twelfth, we can have full employment at fair wages, and it pays for itself.

Thirteenth, there is no need for austerity, at all in that case.

Fourteenth, please go and talk about this. By really understanding something as simple as how money is created - and by being aware that it is never in short supply as a result - we can rebuild from the mess that we are in. We can have the sustainable world we want.

Sorted.

The End.

◆

2. Quantitative easing

I can remember a time when quantitative easing, or QE as it is commonly called, was not a part of my economic thinking. But for more than a decade now QE, and the many issues it gives rise to, has been unavoidable for those who address macroeconomic issues, as I do in my work.

For me that has been especially true. I created the idea of Green QE in 2010[1]. This challenged the then new understanding of what QE might achieve, and how. I already forecast by then that QE would create considerable social and economic division in society. I also suggested that it would not lead to any real new investment in the economy. I think that subsequent events have proved that to be true.

The ideas within Green QE were noticed. Jeremy Corbyn used them as the basis for his economic appeal when successfully seeking to become leader of the Labour Party in 2015. He called the idea People's QE. Otherwise, it was as I proposed it [2] [3].

People's, or Green, QE has not happened, a yet. QE itself most certainly has. In the UK financial year 2020/21 maybe £450 billion of QE will be done – a sum likely to be as big as the government's deficit in that year. Much, if

1 http://www.financeforthefuture.com/GreenQuEasing.pdf
2 https://en.wikipedia.org/wiki/People%27s_Quantitative_Easing
3 https://www.ft.com/content/c1060fb0-41b4-11e5-b98b-87c7270955cf

not all, of the coronavirus crisis will be paid for using QE. That alone makes this an issue that has to be understood.

This thread, which sought to explain the significance of QE, was published on 22 November 2020[4]. It reached almost 400,000 people and has had about 28,000 interactions at the time of writing.

◆

There's massive misunderstanding about what QE is and what it does. So please forgive a long thread on one of the most important tools used in modern economics, which if used properly might provide real hope for a better future.

Outside Japan QE was unknown until 2009. Since then the UK has done £845 billion of it. This is a big deal as a consequence. But as about half of that has happened this year it's appropriate to suggest that there have been two stage of QE, so far. And I suggest we need a third.

Stage 1 QE started in 2009 and was last used in 2016. It created £445bn of new money. That was used to buy £435bn of government bonds, or gilts, and £10bn of corporate bonds, which we can ignore. There were three goals to first stage QE.

The first was to keep interest rates down. The Bank of England calls QE monetary policy for a reason. Buying gilts in the financial markets pushes up their price. And since the return paid on them is fixed if their price goes up the effective interest rate paid on them goes down.

4 https://twitter.com/RichardJMurphy/status/1330492226678513669

The second reasons was to provide liquidity to banks and financial institutions. This liquidity froze in 2008. It was solved because QE created money ends up being held by banks and building societies on the central bank reserve accounts they hold at the Bank of England.

Since 2008 banks and building societies have not trusted each other to not go bust, overnight. After all, Lehman Brothers did. So they don't give each other credit any more. Instead they have to hold central bank reserve account balances to settle their debts to each other.

QE boosted the balances on central bank reserve accounts. In 2009 these amounted to £42bn. In February 2020, when the last audited figure was published, they were £479bn. They have probably gone up by another £400 billion or more by now as a result of QE this year[5].

So, QE provided the money to make sure that the banking system could still function. It should not fall over again in the way it almost did in 2008 as a result, although it had a good go at doing so in March this year[6], which is why the Bank of England intervened so heavily then.

Third, it has to be remembered that QE began in 2009. Back then it was still the official line that banks needed deposits before they could lend. That was not true. It hasn't been since at least 1971. But this was not acknowledged by the Bank of England until 2014.

Given that this 'old world' view on deposits and lending prevailed the BoE thought QE would enable banks to

5 The year 2020/21, that is.
6 March 2020, that is.

lend more to boost the economy. That was nonsense, and the evidence proved it. Creative lending to promote employment remained as rare as ever within UK banking despite QE.

What QE did instead was two things. First, it released money to buy other assets. Speculation in commodities such as oil and metals increased significantly, and even pushed up inflation. But falling interest rates also did something else. It pushed up share prices.

Just as high gilt prices push down gilt interest rates, so too do low interest rates make shares look more attractive and so push up their prices. A steady increase in share prices followed. By 2019 they had roughly doubled since 2009, although they have fallen since[7].

It should be added that there is one big problem with all this money going into shares. Little, if any of it actually ends up in the companies that issue the shares in question. It's just speculative activity in existing shares. It was great for the City, but almost no one else.

The 'almost' in that last sentence was deliberate. QE also benefited the government. Despite the claim that it faced a debt crisis that required austerity the QE programme from 2009 to 2012, totalling £375bn, meant that most government debt in that period was funded by QE.

Let's be clear what 'funded by QE' means. The funding is not direct. All government spending is initially paid for by the Bank of England making payment on

7 True at the time of writing

government command. The overdraft this might create is then by convention cleared by a mix of tax receipts and debt issues.

The debt the government issues to clear a deficit on its account with the Bank of England (which is what the term really means) can last for a few days to more than 50 years. And all of that debt can be traded, or sold, on the City money markets.

People want to own that debt. Banks, building societies, pension funds, life assurance companies, foreign governments, individuals even, all appreciate owning this debt because it's the safest form of saving available in the UK in sterling. UK debt's great stuff that people want.

When QE is used to buy this debt back, because that's what it does, the Bank of England does so using a company called the Bank of England Asset Purchase Facility Fund Limited, or APF for short. This is owned by the Bank of England but, there is a twist.

The APF might be owned by the Bank, but it is effectively controlled by the UK Treasury, which consents in writing to all that it does, including all QE spending. And the Treasury also underwrites all its losses (it has not had many of them) and is entitled to all its profits.

What is more, although the interest on the gilts the APF owns is still paid, the interest actually goes straight back to the Treasury as income, effectively cancelling it, of course. So there are political shenanigans going on here.

The first shenanigan is that the so-called independence of the Bank of England from the Treasury is blown apart by the fact that the Treasury completely controls the APF and the whole QE process. QE is a Treasury operation in practice, not a Bank of England one.

The second shenanigan is that the claim that QE does not cancel debt is blown apart by the fact that repurchased debt is not really owned by the Bank of England but is owned by the Treasury, which gets all the income and profits from it.

Importantly, you can't, of course, owe yourself money. A debt requires that you owe a third party. But the Treasury does not do that, because the government also owns the Bank of England. But how the mechanics of this works needs explanation.

To undertake QE the BoE lends the APF money. Like all bank loans, this one is created out of thin air. The BoE promises to pay whoever the APF instructs it to make payment to. The APF promises to repay the loan. The two promises create the new money that the debt represents.

The APF then uses its new funds to buy gilts. It uses an auction process, paying the market price as a result. The people selling usually profit, often considerably, as a result. After the repurchase the APF legally owns the repurchased gilts, but the Treasury does in reality.

None of the gilts bought by the APF have ever been sold back to financial markets. Such is the scale of likely deficits in the future it is wholly unrealistic to think that they ever will be. So, once the APF buys these gilts it is now reasonable to think that they are cancelled.

The Bank and government do not agree. They say they could be resold. They do this to pretend the debt still exists. They are included in national debt calculations although no one is owed any money. And the interest on them is still treated as a cost to the gov't, which it isn't.

There is only one possible explanation for this pretence, which is that this maintains the austerity narrative. The pretence that there is a debt to repay, and an interest cost to settle, is used as an excuse to cut government spending even though no such excuse exists.

It is appropriate to note what really happens to the money paid by the APF to buy gilts. Even now, when QE is heading to be more than £800 billion, it simply becomes money deposited by the UK's banks and building societies on central bank reserve accounts with the Bank of England.

So the question is whether or not this is a debt? In a normal bank it would be. Customer deposits in normal banks are liabilities. They are money owing to customers that the bank could have to pay out on and find the money to settle. But the Bank of England is not a normal bank.

The deposits UK banks have with the Bank of England only exist because the Bank of England created that money in the first place. And only they, amongst banks, can create money by lending within their own organisation i.e. within government. So this is different from other money.

That difference has real impact. First, the UK's banks can't in effect get rid of these deposits. All they can do is transfer them between themselves. Only government can cancel these deposits, by charging extra tax or selling new bonds and letting the deposits be used to make payment.

In that case these deposits aren't debt. They are, instead, money created by the BoE. And just in case there is doubt as to whether money created by the Bank of England is debt or not, bank notes are not in the ONS national debt figures. So nor should this new money be, either.

Interest is paid on these central bank reserve accounts. It's settled at BoE base rate. That's 0.1% right now. But that's convention. This need not be the case. The Bank of England could change the rules if interest rates rose and there would be nothing banks could do about it.

So, not only under conventional QE is the debt repurchased effectively cancelled, as is the interest on it, but it's replaced by newly created money that is not part of the national debt.

Think about it: government created money can't be part of the national debt because it can only be repaid using more new government created money. That means repayment would create new money exactly equivalent to the amount repaid, so it cannot be debt in any conventional sense.

The result is stage 1 QE benefitted the banks, enormously; lifted asset prices, like shares, considerably; let the government cancel most of its new debt from 2009 to 2012; and left the austerity story completely intact so that most people were economically conned by this.

What has happened in stage 2 of QE, which is the 2020 story? The mechanism is identical is the first thing to say. None of that needs retelling, at all. The figures have just gone up by more than £400 billion all round, that's all.

But the motivation was different. The first stage of this happened in March[8]. As coronavirus lock down happened that month the banks froze. They were back to 2008 and seemingly unwilling to function. £200 billion of new QE then was intended to simply free up the markets.

That worked. Andrew Bailey claimed he was a superhero as a result. Actually, he just did his job as creator of new money, which is what the markets needed to unblock the jam that was created as banks thought they faced Armageddon.

But the £200 billion also did something else. As it became obvious government deficits would skyrocket new QE provided all the funds required for markets to acquire the new debt the government was issuing, and at the same time still keep interest rates low.

Literally, what the QE process did was pump money into the financial markets as a result of the repurchase of gilts, which money was then available to buy the new

8 March 2020

gilts the government had to offer because of significant deficit spending.

The difference between stage 1 and stage 2 QE then becomes clear. In stage 1 there could be a pretence that the QE funds were part of monetary policy to control interest rates. They just happened, coincidentally to effectively cancel government debt as well.

In stage 2 QE, for anyone with the willingness to look at what was really happening it was apparent that the Bank of England was actually deliberately creating the funds required to fund government spending in advance of them being needed. It was as simple as that.

With £450 billion of QE planned for 2020/21 and an anticipated deficit of around £400 billion when allowance is made for the profit many gilt owners make in reselling their bonds to the government is taken into account the Bank of England is almost wholly funding the deficit.

So, when the question is asked 'who is lending money to the government right now?' The answer is 'No one'. Instead every penny of the deficit is being paid for with newly created money that is being provided by the Bank of England. And national debt is not in rising as a result.

Of course, the newly created money goes somewhere. It ends up in the central bank reserve accounts held with the Bank of England by the UK's banks and building societies. These are likely worth more than £800 billion now. All earning interest at 0.1%.

There is a good question to ask about why these banks earn 0.1% on money they did not seek. But that's for another day. More important is the fact that in net terms in Stage 2 QE there is no money to reinvest elsewhere in the economy.

That's because the markets effectively sold no gilts back to the government. Unlike Stage 1 QE, in Stage 2 QE the overall impact is that the Bank of England is simply funding new gilt issues. It's directly funding the government. The markets are almost removed from the equation.

This is not, in that case, monetary policy, even if it does keep interest rates low. This is fiscal policy, in effect. This is about deficit financing. The pretence that the BoE does QE for monetary policy reasons is shattered. It is not. Nor is it in any way independent.

We have reached the point where in reality the claim that the government cannot borrow from its central bank is shown to be a myth. It is doing just that, with the Bank using newly created money that ends up on central bank reserve accounts, to do so.

But this also means that there is no argument for austerity. There is no new debt. And no one is owed anything to repay the central bank reserve account balances, because they are just money. And until there is full employment this new money creation creates no risk of inflation.

So, any claim that we are suffering under a mountain of debt is just wrong. If anything, because of the scale of gilt repurchased national debt is at most stable in amount. It might actually be going down.

Stage 2 QE is not, however, what is prescribed by modern monetary theory. None of the artificial structures that QE uses are in any way required by MMT. It says that the Bank of England should actually just run an overdraft for the government, which is what is really happening.

But whether Stage 2 QE is what modern monetary theory would prescribe is not the point. MMT does explain what is happening. A government in the situation we face in 2020 can fund itself using new money creation. That is exactly what is happening.

Crucially, there is no debt as a result. There is only new money. The amount of that money is wholly under government control. And there is no inflation risk at this moment. Not need there be, external shocks like Brexit apart. This is a completely stable situation.

So, tales that borrowing has reached its limits and that austerity is required, or that we are saddling future generations with debt are all nonsense. No one can, or needs to, repay the new money the government has created. But the government has to understand that.

If the government does not understand this it can do something catastrophic. It can increase overall tax, which would crush demand in the economy, and so increase unemployment. Or it can cut spending, which has the same result.

The government can suck the lifeblood out of the economy, in other words. By choosing to believe its own austerity narrative it can deliver an economic disaster. George Osborne had a good go at this. Rishi Sunak might try to do so again.

What should the government do? Stage 3 QE is my answer. This is quite different to stages 1 and 2. In stages 1 and 2 there's no direct link between government spending and QE. It's indirect. Spend creates the deficit, requiring bonds to clear it, which requires QE to cancel them.
In Stage 3 QE the link to spending is explicit. In this stage the government plans economic recovery. Call it a Green New Deal. A Green or National Investment Bank funds this programme. It issues bonds to pay for the investment. The Bank of England uses QE to but those bonds.

Now QE is explicitly created in advance to fund spending. It does not mop up after the event. It is used to provide some of the money needed to transform our economy. This does not mean other savers cannot provide funds as well. I have argued that this option should be available.

But, the intention is to show that a lack of private sector and private saver willingness to fund the economic transformation we need to recover and sustain our economy should not prevent that transformation taking place. Government has the power to make this change happen.

That power comes from its ability to create money for social benefit. This has been used so far to save our banks, and to fund COVID created deficits. Now it could be used to fund the transition to a sustainable economy we need if no other sources are available.

The government should try to secure capital required from other sources, by all means. But doing so is not a constraint. For a government in the position of the UK government, a lack of money is not a constraint. How much money there is in the economy is its to decide.

Of course it has to consider inflation. That can be controlled if it is economically rather than politically created (the latter being of the sort Brexit will deliver) by additional taxes, bond sales, or cuts in spending. But we have no risk of that type of inflation right now.

So Stage 3 QE could deliver the recovery we so desperately need, if linked to investment, in particular.

What is necessary is that the power of QE be understood. Few have tried to do that. There are few politicians in that number. But it's time QE - or the power to create money - was understood. Because this is how we control and deliver the economy of the future.

◆

3. QE and funding the Green New Deal

This thread was posted on 28 November 2020[1] and was a follow up to the one in the previous chapter because people wanted to know more about how QE related to funding the Green New Deal, which is another initiative I have been involved in[2] since co-authoring the very first version in 2008.

As a follow up it did not get as many reads as the previous chapter, but I feel it is worth including here because it makes clear how intimately linked these ideas and the mechanisms for tackling our climate and biodiversity crises are. That fact has been better appreciated in the USA than the UK at present, but we will need to get to that point as well.

◆

I've tweeted more about quantitative easing than I really thought to be decent of late. However, the questions still keep coming, so here is another QE thread, on the use of QE funds and (especially) the link to the Green New Deal...

1 https://twitter.com/RichardJMurphy/status/1332645218152312834
2 https://greennewdealgroup.org/

The question I have been asked is does it matter what QE money is spent on, and the honest answer is 'it's complicated'. But, maybe not so complicated if it's understood that QE came in three stages, each of which is quite different.

Stage 1 QE lasted from 2009 until 2016, when the last round of this stage took place in the UK. The aim at this stage was simple. As always, new money was created by the Bank of England, and government bonds (gilts) were bought with that money, in the main. That's what QE does, in essence.

Stage 1 QE had the aim of removing gilts from the market. The idea was that money would go as a result into riskier assets, and new investment. It didn't. It went into speculation. But interest rates were kept low. And banks got new money, and that protected them from failure.

In Stage 1 QE the government also in effect got funds to cover its deficit. But to be clear, QE did not fund the government's spending in this period. That was never the intention, and never what happened. Stage 1 (and 2) QE mopped up the debt that spending had already created.

That QE only mops up debt is not surprising. As modern monetary theory makes clear, all government spending starts with money creation. And then the overdraft this, in effect, creates at the Bank of England is cleared by tax receipts or debt. But the debt never comes first. So it never funds the spend.

Stage 2 QE emerged in 2020. Unlike Stage 1 the aim was not to redirect where the City put their money. The aim was to make sure that financial markets were not going to be overwhelmed by having to buy the large number of new gilts that would otherwise be on sale. It's worked.

Stage 2 QE has other aims as well. Keeping interest rates low was still necessary. And protecting banks from stress in financial turmoil remained a priority, and key in March 2020. But primarily this was a debt funding exercise. And the spend still came first.

I'm not sure I can stress this enough: Stages 1 and 2 QE did not fund government spending. The government can do that any time it wants. It has its own bank. But because it thinks it has to clear its overdraft with the Bank of England it has to issue debt.

The only reason for Stages 1 and 2 QE is debt management, and not to fund spending. Stage 1 QE aimed to make government debt less attractive by lowering interest rates, to supposedly force money elsewhere. Stage 2 provides a buyer for the debt the market may not want right now.

It is only what I call Stage 3 QE that might change the use of QE money. I developed this idea in 2010. It was called Green Quantitative Easing back then. Jeremy Corbyn called it People's QE. John McDonnell was scared of it. It's quite different to Stage 1 & 2 QE.

In Stage 3 QE a government owned investment bank seeks to secure funding to transform an economy. The aim is to deliver a Green New Deal, and everything that goes with it. I stress this could be done by conventional government spending. Plus Stage 2 QE. But Stage 3 QE is better.

Stage 3 is about much more than QE though. It recognises that vast amounts of saving is wasted right now. The stock market and land speculation are just Ponzi schemes that don't deliver added value new jobs. Cash sits uselessly in bank accounts. Savings need to work.

Stage 3 QE works alongside a transformation of savings. State subsidies to savings - that drive the Ponzi scheme arrangements we have - need to change. So pensions funds, to get tax relief, must save 25% of their new contributions in investments that create new green employment.

The Stage 3 QE job creating investments in green jobs can be in the private sector, of course. They need not be in the UK. After all, this is a global issue. But the point is the only real useful long term investments we have now are in the green economy - so that investment needs to happen.

Stage 3 QE also requires that ISA savings be changed. £70bn a year goes into ISAs. Some is reinvestment, but it's still a massive sum. And all that money needs to go into guaranteed green savings bonds issued by a National Investment Bank where it could fund the Green New Deal.

Do what I have said to reform tax on savings and all the money required to fund a Green New Deal may be found. We may not need Stage 3 QE for this purpose at all in that case. But what if the need for reform is bigger than the capacity of savings to fund? Then Stage 3 QE can kick in.

To make Stage 3 QE work the National Investment Bank issues bonds and then the Bank of England acquires them in the usual QE way — effectively making money available for green investment. Now, for the first time, QE might be linked to an actual spend.

The link between the spend by the National Investment Bank and QE is always going to be at a distance though. The Bank of England is still playing its role of mopping up debt in this Stage 3 approach to QE. It does not control the spend. It does not manage it. It just buys debt.

It's really important to say this. QE, whether in Stages 1, 2 or 3, never gives the Bank of England control of spending. That always stays wholly under the control of the government in Stages 1 and 2, and the government owned National Investment Bank in Stage 3.

In conclusion, QE does not fund or direct spending. It is a way of managing debt. That's it. But we do need ways of managing debt right now. And QE - which meets international requirements and lets the Bank of England indirectly fund the government - is critical right now.

◆

4. How to use local and hypothecated bonds to fund the recovery

This chapter is one of the two in this book which did not get published as a Twitter thread. It was instead posted on my blog[1] on 26 January 2021. However, because it builds on themes in the previous section on QE, saving and the Green New Deal I thought it important to include it here. What it seeks to demonstrate is that we can afford the society we both want, and as importantly, need.

◆

I made a suggestion recently[2] that it is now essential to the restoration of balance within the UK economy that the accumulating pile of savings that the last decade has created should be directed towards social and productive purpose when that is not the case at present.

To give some illustration, wealth has increased dramatically over the past decade. As indication, maybe £70 billion

1 https://www.taxresearch.org.uk/Blog/2021/01/26/how-to-use-local-and-hypothecated-bond-issues-to-fund-the-recovery/
2 See Chapter 3

a year goes into ISAs, and more than £100 billion a year into pensions[3]. The tax subsidy to achieve these contributions costs almost £60 billion a year. In itself that is a cause for asking why a social dimension is not required with regard to these savings, but there is another aspect to this.

Savings have not just gone up because of the sums saved. The extraordinary increases in wealth cannot have happened for this reason alone. Instead, they have also happened because of the deficits that the government has run over the last decade.

Those deficits have been necessary and appropriate. Indeed, they may well have been too small. But they had an inevitable consequence. When the government runs a deficit someone else has to run a surplus. That's a fact dictated by double-entry accounting. The sectoral balances show this. This is the latest UK version[4], from the Office for Budget Responsibility:

Chart 2.31: Sectoral net lending

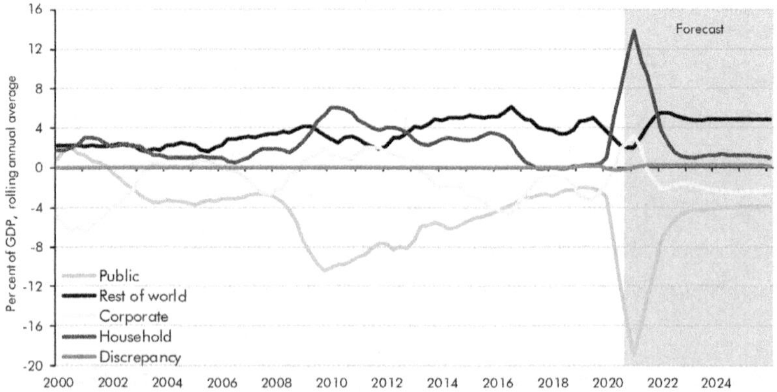

Source: ONS, OBR

3 https://www.taxresearch.org.uk/Blog/2019/12/06/funding-the-green-new-deal-how-we-could-save-for-the-planet/

4 https://obr.uk/download/economic-and-fiscal-outlook-november-2020/ Since updated in March 2021

As deficits go up so too do savings. And so, the stock of savings in the UK has grown.

This has had an exponential consequence. Since almost all this saving has gone into land, housing or shares, all of which are kept in deliberately short supply by markets keen to maximise profit, the prices of those assets have risen, considerably. The result has been an even greater increase in wealth than there has been in savings. This is data from the ONS[5] from April 2020:

Breakdown of total aggregate wealth by component (£ trillion)	July 2006 to June 2008	July 2008 to June 2010	July 2010 to June 2012	July 2012 to June 2014	July 2014 to June 2016	April 2016 to March 2018
Property Wealth (net)	3.54	3.38	3.53	3.81	4.52	5.09
Financial Wealth (net)	1.04	1.09	1.31	1.56	1.63	2.12
Physical Wealth	0.96	1.02	1.08	1.13	1.23	1.32
Private Pension Wealth	2.89	3.47	3.53	4.39	5.35	6.10
Total Wealth (including Private Pension Wealth)	8.43	8.96	9.44	10.89	12.73	14.63
Total Wealth (excluding Private Pension Wealth)	5.54	5.49	5.91	6.50	7.38	8.53
GDP	1.57	1.56	1.67	1.81	1.93	2.09

I am sure that not much has changed since then in terms of the trend.

But there is a problem here. QE, rightly or wrongly, has been in use for a decade now. And what QE does, quite deliberately, is to force money out of safe bonds and into speculative investment, so pushing up the price of both with the intended aim of reducing effective interest rates. It does then, effectively, inject hot money to fuel speculative activity into the economy.

There are massive consequences of this. One is the resulting enormous increase in financial wealth, as noted above, and so an increase in inequality.

5 https://www.ons.gov.uk/releases/wealthingreatbritainwave62016to2018
6 https://www.sheffield.ac.uk/polopoly_fs/1.892482!/file/Against-Hollow-Firms.pdf

Another has been an increase in the return to speculation that has discouraged any form of real investment, at cost to real production and jobs within the economy[6].

The third is to create a complete disconnect between financial markets and real investment return.

Fourth there is always a risk that the financial markets might crash, simply making overall economic wellbeing worse, and not better.

And fifth, whilst all this is going on, many quite reasonably resent it and become alienated from society and politics which they correctly see as offering them very little of real consequence, whilst the returns to a few rise exponentially. This is a recipe for the social breakdowns that we are now witnessing politically.

My remedy is to address the disconnect between savings and investment in society. My logic is as follows.

First, there is a massive investment shortfall in society if we are to meet current needs for new infrastructure as well as creating the transition to sustainability that we require.

Second, we need this investment to deliver the recovery that is now required post-Covid.

Third, the subsidy that the state gives to the already wealthy by providing them with incentives to save must be applied for social gain. It's hard to imagine a counterargument.

Fourth, inequality must be tackled. Even the IMF and OECD now say so.

Fifth, we must seek to avoid a financial crash which continuing QE of the type now used might promote.

Sixth, further QE of that type plus any increase in tax or borrowing must be avoided, as all work against achievement of the above objectives.

Seventh, so too does simple money injection work against that objective since it too increases the sectoral imbalances and does therefore increase savings, whether that is the intention or not, meaning that modern monetary theory has not got all the answers on this.

Which means we have to do something more radical, which is to now reconnect savings, and those that we subsidise through the tax system in particular, and the real economy by encouraging the rather novel (as it turns out) idea that savings might be used as capital to fund the investment that we need for the benefit of all in society.

Doing this is easy. As I have noted, the relationship between tax reliefs and savings in the UK is very marked. Something like 80% of all private wealth is saved in tax incentivised assets[7], whether that be pension funds, ISAs, other tax driven schemes, and housing, which is massively tax subsidised by being free of capital gains tax.

7 https://www.cambridge.org/core/journals/social-policy-and-society/article/modern-monetary-theory-and-the-changing-role-of-tax-in-society/B7A8B0C7C80C8F7E38D20BE4F5099C83

So, my suggestion is that ISAs must only be allowed in future if the ISA funds are invested in bonds that in turn fund activities that can be shown, without doubt, to produce new jobs that support the required transformation of the UK.

I also suggest that 25% of all new (not existing) pension contributions should be required to be invested in the same way.

Together these two measures could result in maybe £100 billion a year of capital being available for investment in the UK, which is more than enough to fund the Green New Deal (which the Climate Change Committee thinks might cost £60 billion a year) and ample other social investment as well, whilst freeing government revenue budgets to address other vital issues, like health, care, education and justice issues.

How could this investment programme be achieved in practice? I suggest that hypothecated bonds be issued. These could be regional (big enough to be effective, but small enough to be local e.g. East Anglia or South Wales) or they could be activity focussed e.g. health, housing, the Green New Deal, and so on. There is no reason not to do both, and mix the benefits.

The bonds would be invested for the use for which they were subscribed. But the investment projects and their amounts would be set by government. So investment limits may have to be set, and government should also make good shortfalls: this should not be a rationing mechanism. Third stage QE could make up any shortfalls if a region requires additional funding[8].

As important, the interest rate should be the same for all funds, and be both attractive in the market (above average, towards top end for the periods offered, and locking up funds for a period would be part of the deal) and guaranteed by the government. It could also be tax free, as ISAs are.

Redemption should always be possible. Normal circulation should cover this issue. If not QE could. This would be Green QE in that case, because the funds would then be linked to a specific purpose and not be randomly allocated within markets[9].

Long term capital redemption would be funded by renting assets created to the government. If funds were made available to the private sector (and they might be, via a National Investment Bank, acting like a venture capital fund) they would obviously be expected to pay a return.

And the interest would be guaranteed by government. Suppose the rate might be 1%. On £100 billion that's a £1 billion annual cost. Let's not over-sweat the cost in that case. Putting a cap on balances that might be held in these accounts (less than £500,000 I would suggest, and maybe more like £100,000) would make sure that not too much of this is captured by the already wealthy.

8 See the previous chapter
9 See the previous chapter

So why do this? Because it solves the problems I note, which are real, politically, socially and economically.

And why do this, rather than do existing bonds as I have been asked? Simply because these existing bonds might be economically 'efficient' but they create the social, political and economic consequences I note. Efficiency is a very long way from being the criteria for success in the political economy that I care about.

So will they work? In terms of attracting funds I have not a shadow of a doubt. I think people would be queueing to get them.

In terms then of freeing the government to fund other activities, I again have not a doubt.

In terms or promoting an awareness of the relationship between savings and investment, that will depend on the marketing and reporting. It will be vital that people think there is a relationship between their savings and outcomes. Good reporting will then be vital.

And in terms of additional funding for investment? I am sure that will happen.

Whilst tax reliefs will be better spent.

And two other things will be achieved. Savers are older. Those who will get work from this will mainly be younger. This activity could promote inter-generational solidarity in that case, which is now vital.

In the process it could also underpin what I call the real pension contract (explained here[10]) which requires inter-generational transfers of income and wealth.

We will also get a Green New Deal, better housing, schools, hospitals, transport and other infrastructure. And by freeing government budgets for alternative use other than funding investment we will end up with better services too.

We could even have full employment. And for those who worry about such things, balanced budgets follow on from full employment.

Now, what is not to like?

◆

10 https://www.taxresearch.org.uk/Blog/2019/08/28/getting-the-fundamental-pension-contract-right/

5. Debt

I posted this thread on 20 December 2020[1]. Since then it has reached 215,000 people and more than 25,000 people have engaged with it.

The motivation for the post was simple: it was to explain why the national debt – about which the UK media and its politicians obsess – is not the issue that they portray it to be. I go so far as to suggest that the debt is not only useful, but repaying it makes no sense at all.

◆

I am bemused by those who demand that we repay the UK government's debt. It makes me wonder, do they know what it is? And how do they think it can be repaid? And do they appreciate the consequences? A thread is coming on... bear with me, because I think you need to know this.

First, what is the UK government's debt? I've immersed myself in this issue and can confidently say the Office for National Statistic's figures are wrong, most especially because they claim that the UK government is in debt by owing money to itself. That's not possible.

Whatever the Office for National Statistics like to claim, money you owe yourself is not debt, and so quantitative easing cancels about £800 billion of UK national debt

1 https://twitter.com/RichardJMurphy/status/1340619006412288003

right now[2]. There are other mistakes in their numbers, but I'll just stick with this one for the moment.

So, if the ONS claim the national debt is around £2.1 trillion at present, it isn't. Allowing for the UK government owning around £800 billion of its own debt the figure reduces to maybe £1.3 trillion, give or take a bit. But that, I hasten to add, is not the end of the story.

It's important to understand that the ONS includes some things few would think of as debt in their figures. For example, around £200 billion (£0.2 trillion) of National Savings balances are included in the national debt. Whoever knew Premium Bond holders were such a burden?

Come to that, in reality the remaining gilts are, when all is said and done, just savings accounts. They are simply the safest place for long term savers like pension funds, life assurance companies and foreign governments to place their money.

The question that has to be asked then is why when the government spends more than £60bn a year subsidising pension, ISA and other saving (as it does) is it so desperate that this money be saved anywhere but with the government itself? That simply makes no sense.

So all who claim they are desperate to repay the national debt should really be asked, why are you so keen to stop people saving in the safest way they can? Because that's what they are really demanding should

2 See Chapter 2

happen. And there's no evidence people want to stop saving that way.

And remember, government backed saving is so popular that right now people will buy government gilts, or bonds, due to be repaid in 40 years time with a negative interest rate, which means they will get back less than they actually save now. And people still buy it.

In that case there is another question for those complaining about debt, which is why are they so obsessed about the debt when the cost of interest on it as at a record low, and still falling, and in absolute terms costs less a year than it did before the 2008 crash?

On gilts and national savings, which together make up most of the 'debt', the questions to debt obsessives is then, why don't they want people to save with the government when that's what they really very badly want to do? Why deny people what the savings market wants?

The other issue to understand about the national debt is what happens to the figure that replaces QE when QE cancels government debt because the government can't owe itself? That replacement figure is what are called central bank reserve account balances, or CBRAs, for short.

Central bank reserve accounts have around £800 billion held on them right now, and that number is growing. That figure's not the same as the QE balance, but there is a relationship between the two. And that's for good reason.

When the government buys back its own debt when doing QE it creates new money within the Bank of England to do this. There's nothing mysterious about it doing so. All banks create new money by lending, and the BoE makes a loan to a subsidiary company to create this money.

Then that subsidiary company uses the money it's had created for it to buy back the government's own debt. And to record that fact the payment made has to go through the central bank reserve accounts that the UK's commercial banks maintain with the Bank of England.

It's important to note that CBRAs are only available to commercial banks. That's because they are the accounts used to move money between commercial banks and the government. There is nothing mysterious about this. They just are what they are: a collection of bank accounts.

And remember, all that bank accounts do is record debts. All money in the modern world is debt. It's nothing else. And so all that a bank account does is record who has agreed to owe who else money. It's hard to get this essential point, but vital to do so.

So, when the government agrees with someone to buy the gilts, or government bonds, that they own then a payment must follow. And since all payments from the government go into the rest of the economy via the commercial banks then the CBRAs have to go up to record this payment.

Now here's the hard bit. For most people it's mind-blowing. When the commercial banks now pay their customers the money the government owes them the balances in the CBRAs do not change. The balances between the commercial banks and their customers do but the CBRAs are not altered.

People want to think that it's money from the government that's used to pay the banks' customers. Of course, in a sense it is. But the CBRA remains untouched by the transaction. And this needs explanation.

That explanation is easy. When the government pays a commercial bank the money due for the gilts that payment does not benefit the bank. It benefits the bank's customer. So the double entry in the commercial bank is to debit the CBRA and to credit the bank customer's account.

The bank is in this sense a genuine intermediary. And all they are doing is some accounting. There are no piles of notes that change hands, let alone gold or any other such tangible thing. Money is debt. So all the bank is doing is recording changes in debts owing.

As a result of this transaction the Bank of England now owes the commercial bank more money. And the commercial bank owes its customer as a result. But when the customer then spends that money the CBRA does not change. The Bank of England still owes the commercial bank money.

The promise to pay the Bank of England makes to the commercial bank is reflected in that bank's CBRA. The promise to pay that the commercial bank makes to its customer is reflected in that customer's account. There are two promises to pay and two accounts. They're not related.

Understand those last few tweets and you understand modern banking, and very few people do. Sadly, almost none of our politicians seem to do so.

But what does this mean for the national debt? If we now have, as a result of QE, the government owning its own bonds and the Bank of England owing commercial banks a roughly similar amount instead, is the government still in debt for the value of the debts QE has cancelled?

The answer, at one level, has to be that yes, it is. If all money is debt and the Bank of England, which is owned by the government, is in debt to the commercial banks then surely it follows that the government is in debt? Superficially that seems to be true.

But then think about this a bit more. What is that sum now owing on the Central Bank Reserve Accounts that in reality now makes up about £800 billion of the supposed national debt? It is simply money. And what is more, it's money made by the Bank of England.

So, that money is something very like bank notes in some ways. After all, they are what we also call money. And they are also created by the Bank of England. And, just for the record, as my forthcoming research has shown, they are not included in the national debt.

There is a good reason to not include this government created money - what is called 'base money' - in the national debt. That's because base money, which is banknotes and central bank reserve account balances, is what the Bank of England call 'the ultimate means of settlement'.

In other words, base money is the means of payment when all else fails, which is why commercial banks now need so much of it to make sure that they can function and always pay each other and why cash is also the ultimate backstop for payment in the economy when or if trust fails.

And if something is the 'ultimate means of settlement' then how can it be repaid, except by using itself? After all, this is money. That is the only available description of it that there is. That's what the Bank of England says it creates when doing QE.

So, what those demanding that the UK national debt be repaid are really saying is that this Bank of England money that keeps our economy functioning must be repaid. But what does that mean? Indeed, what is repayment of any of the supposed national debt going to mean?

First of all, let's make clear that the government bonds that have been repurchased by the government using QE can't be repaid. There is simple reason for that. They have, in effect, already been repaid. They have been cancelled in all but name. They need not be discussed again.

Then let's consider National Savings savings accounts, like Premium Bonds, which form part of the national debt. Can I presume that no one is suggesting that these accounts must actually be closed to clear the national debt? If so, let's live with this £200bn of savings some call debt.

Now let's consider the remaining gilts, or bonds in issue. Many of these are used, just like National Savings accounts, to provide a safe place for money to be saved. Can I presume that no one wants to take away safe savings accounts? Why would you? So, let's keep that part.

Another pile of gilts are owned by banks and others as a result of regulation that requires that they have access to ultra-safe money. The object is to present another bank crash. Can I presume no one wants another bank crash? So, let's keep those gilts in issue.

A significant chunk of gilts - around £400bn or so - are owned by foreign governments. That's because they want to own sterling, and this is how they do it. They see gilts as being as good as money. There is good reason for that. Gilts really are the next best thing to money.

My guess is that we don't want to force foreign governments to sell their UK government bond holdings because that might create a currency crisis which won't help the UK. I doubt anyone wants one of them. So, let's leave those gilts well alone too in that case.

Who else owns gilts? Banks do. They use them to underpin what is called the repo market. This is not the place to explain that market in detail. But in essence it is used to guarantee the safety of money deposited in UK banks by very large companies, usually overnight.

Most UK savers who have what they think to be 'money in the bank' enjoy a government guarantee to make sure it is repaid. In that case I guess they won't want to deny large companies the chance to also have a guarantee on their savings. So, these gilts are also needed.

So, what's left to the gilt markets that might be repaid after we take all these factors into account? Not a lot to be candid. So why the obsession about repaying these gilts? It is really hard to fathom.

In fact, the only thing to say about the desire to force gilt repayment is that it is wholly destructive. It would undermine the pensions, savings, life assurance, foreign exchange and banking sectors. There are left wingers who might want this. But why anyone else? I'm baffled.

I am also baffled by the desire to force gilt repayment when there seems some desire on the part of the financial markets to own more of them. I have no clue why so many who describe themselves as market fundamentalists are so anxious to deny markets what they want.

There appears to be a self-destruct instinct in those commentators who want the national debt repaid because their beloved City could barely function without it. Do they not realise? Do they not know? Are they lying? Or do they just hate the state so much that they don't care?

Whatever the reason that people want gilts repaid is, let's move on to the £800bn on central bank reserve accounts that they also want cleared. How could that be repaid? And what will the consequences of an attempt to make this repayment be?

Remember, that this debt is just balances on bank accounts. But these are a peculiar type of bank account. They are, like all bank account balances, debt. But unlike all others, the balances on central bank reserve accounts are deliberately created to function as money.

That's because whilst these balances are technically repayable to any bank on demand, repayment on demand by the Bank of England to one bank means that the sum due to it by another bank increases. That's because electronic money has to be redeposited. That's double entry at work.

To reiterate: this redepositing has to happen. Unlike cash, central bank reserve account balances can't be lost down the back of sofas. So, if a bank draws on its own central bank reserve account it inevitably does so to make payment to another bank's central bank reserve account.

That's because this is the way post-2008 that banks deal with each other. They don't trust each other not to fail. So they always demand immediate payment. And if there's a shortage of liquidity to make these payments - as in March 2020 - QE creates more of it, instantly.

So, and to be blunt, it is these balances that are keeping the banking system functioning right now. And as was proved early in 2020, we really do need hundreds of billions of pounds in such accounts, effectively created by the Bank of England via QE, to let banking function.

So why would anyone who does not want a banking crisis want these balances repaid when they play such an enormous role in the functioning of the UK economy, and the City of London? I am utterly baffled to know why. They either want a financial crisis, or don't understand banking.

But let's despite the absurdity of that wish assume that they got their way and it was decided to reduce these balances. This thought experiment is really important. Stick with me, please.

The central bank reserve accounts are debt that can only be cleared by repaying the debt. The commercial banks can't do that. The debt is base money, and not the commercial money that they create. They can't get rid of base money by themselves. Only the government can.

How can the government get rid of base money, which is what the balances on central bank reserve accounts represent? There is only one way, but three mechanisms. The way is to take money out of the economy. The mechanisms are tax increases, bond sales and austerity.

The first two mechanisms mean people pay more money to the government. That additional money payment would have to go to the government through the central bank reserve accounts - that's the only available transmission mechanism. And so the balances on them would reduce.

The third mechanism - austerity - means cutting government spending. If done whilst keeping tax and bond sales (or flows to government savings accounts) constant this reduces the flow of government money into the economy and so reduces the central bank reserve account balances.

Let's ignore that this would mean banks having fewer funds available to them, and all that means. Let's instead consider what a tax increase means. What a tax increase does is take money out of the economy - the reduction in the central bank reserve account balances shows that.

That clears the debt on the central bank reserve accounts, so those demanding this happen get their way. But there's now less money in the real economy we all live in. And that reduction means there is reduced spending power in that economy. And that means demand falls.

Falling demand always has the same outcomes. It means a decline in growth. That in turn means lower sales in businesses. And lower profits. And that then means reduced employment, which in turn means less tax is paid. Which means money does not flow to government the way it did.

A government wanting to reduce the balances on the central bank reserve accounts faces a dilemma in that case. Tax increases are not neutral. Tax increases can reduce economic activity. And that can reduce revenues. But, it has to be stressed, that depends on the tax increased.

So, for example, taxes on wealth do not reduce demand as much as taxes on the incomes or spending of the lowest paid. That's because the wealthy pay taxes out of savings. Low earners have to cut their spend or take on precarious borrowing to pay. Not all taxes are equal then.

But, whatever happens, increasing taxes usually suppresses economic activity. Sometimes that's desirable. However, few see that as being at all likely over the next few years. So why increase taxes then, when the outcome will be bad for the whole economy? I can't answer that.

So what about extra bond sales then? This means selling the bonds the government reacquired when doing QE back into the financial markets. Think of it as QE in reverse. It's discussed often. And it works, in one way. It would reduce the central bank reserve accounts.

There is one problem with reversing QE though. It could be called 'the glaringly obvious'. This is that increasing bonds in issue to clear the central bank reserve accounts does not clear the national debt. It just shifts debt from being due as money, to being due as a bond.

Understanding that QE just simply shifts debt around is no bad thing, because it's true. But given that money (which is what the central bank reserve accounts are) is not the same thing as savings (which is what gilts or bonds are) that does not mean that QE does nothing.

QE had a purpose. It was to reduce interest rates, which has been good news for households in debt. And it reduced the cost of business borrowing too, which means many businesses that might have gone bust of late will not be doing so. That's pretty good news too.

QE had other benefits. As already noted, QE basically created the central bank reserve accounts that have provided the liquidity that banks have needed to keep paying each other without risk of a bank collapse. Staving off a banking crisis is some achievement. QE did that.

Not that I'm saying there are no downsides to QE. There are. Because the funds injected into the banking system were effectively unregulated much simply went into speculation. Stock markets have skyrocketed. The City has won more than anyone else from QE. No one sought that.

There has also been a real downside to this upside for the City from QE. QE has undoubtedly created greater inequality in the UK, and elsewhere come to that. Much of that has been disguised. Governments have been able to claim their economies have recovered. But at a real cost.

This cost of QE has been suffered by those who have been left behind by QE. Reversing QE will not change that, any more than it will reduce the national debt. The redistribution upward has happened. It can't be undone now by shuffling the new wealth distribution around a bit.

So, new bond sales created by reversing QE will not address the problems within the economy, and nor will it reduce the national debt. And tax increases will be really harmful. So we're back to austerity as the only option. And that policy that has failed for the last decade.

Austerity seeks to reduce the flows from government to the rest of the economy through the central bank reserve accounts whilst hoping that tax revenues and the inward flow of funds to the government do not stall. It always was a naive assumption. It still is.

The government is the biggest spender in the UK economy. It's also the biggest employer. And the biggest supplier of savings accounts. The assumption that somehow it can change its behaviour in one way - cutting spend, for example - and leave everything else as it was, is absurd.

Austerity cuts the flow of government created money into the economy. The impact is much the same as a tax cut. Demand in the economy is reduced. So employment falls, and so does tax revenue. But austerity is like a very targeted tax increase. And it hits the least well off hardest.

That the least well off should be hit hardest by austerity should be obvious. The biggest parts of government spend are on the sick, the elderly, those with disability, those on low incomes and the young. Of course they are the least well off. Austerity inevitably harms them all.

Austerity can reduce balances on the central bank reserve accounts. That is indisputable. But the fall in the central bank reserve accounts is not as big as the cuts made because of falling tax revenues and savings inflows to government. And is the cost a price worth paying? No.

So let me summarise this long thread. It's claimed that we need to reduce the national debt. But first of all, we need to state it correctly in numerical terms. And then we need to understand what makes it up.

Roughly half the national debt is made up of gilts or government bonds when those gilts that the government already owns are taken out of account. And these bonds are just savings accounts, in effect.

But these savings have a massively important role in the economy because the holders of these accounts know that the government can never fail to repay these accounts. That's because the government can always create the money to repay. That repayment is guaranteed then.

And in the world post-2008 the ability to repay is fundamental. The trust that existed before then has gone. We know banks crash now. Those demanding gilts be repaid ignore this. They are living in a fantasy past.

In the real present gilts underpin the smooth operation of banking, pensions, many savings products and foreign exchange markets. Since each of these is pretty darned important to the UK suggesting that bonds be repaid is akin to economic madness.

And it's also mad to say that cancelling National Savings is a good idea, and yet around £200 billion of national debt is in this form.

But the craziest demand of all is that we get rid of the money that now underpins the smooth operation of our entire economy, whether by tax increases or austerity, given that bond sakes don't work for this purpose. But then, as I have noted, nor do tax increases or austerity either.

So, what do we do? If repaying the national debt is undesirable, what next? There are four simple things to say here.

First, celebrate the fact that something that is a legacy from the gold standard era of money - which the national debt is - has morphed into something so multi-facetedly useful in the modern money era. Thank goodness that we have it.

Second, stop thinking this 'debt' needs to be repaid. The whole reason it exists is that people absolutely trust that the government can always repay it but quite emphatically do not want them to do so. Its virtue is that it continues to offer safe savings opportunities.

Third, stop all talk of 'our grandchildren having to repay this debt'. That's utter nonsense. They too will need it to make the economy work. And the lucky ones will own some of it, because the national debt is private wealth. The real issue is, how can some more have some of it?

And last, stop worrying about the size of the national debt and instead ask whether we are using it wisely. The question is not whether the national debt is a problem, because of itself it is not. The question is whether or not the policies that change it are the best available.

If austerity is not wise - and it is not - and many tax increases might be destructive right now - what spending and tax policies do we really need to deliver national prosperity? That is the real big issue for current debate.

So now let's come to my last point. Debate on debt repayment exists for a reason. It's not that deep down anyone really wants to repay the so-called national debt. But those promoting debt repayment do so to stop us thinking about what the state can really do for us. The state could promote full employment if there was no debt obsession. It could also reduce inequality. It could consider a basic income. It could deliver a Green New Deal. All of these, and more, are possible. The state could care, in a word.

But those promoting debt repayment try to stop these things that would benefit most people in the country happening by promoting a false, and deeply harmful obsession with the so-called national debt. I hate to say it, but that's because they don't want the state to care.

The national debt is really no such thing. It's actually savings and money. The real job is to spend those sums wisely. Let's move on and talk about that, and so show that we do care.

But that's for another day.

The end.

6. The national debt paranoia

This thread was posted on 2 March 2021, which was the day before the UK Budget. Unusually it had been written more than two weeks beforehand, but I had then put it aside as I was not sure I was happy with it.

In anticipation of the Budget I gave it another look, tweaked it a little, and put it out[1].

It was the right thing to do. The resulting thread addressed issues already noted in the previous chapter, with some differences of emphasis, but this one is the most successful thread in this book. It has reached more than 1.7 million people and more than 130,000 have interacted with it.

The moral may be that I need to give Tweets a little time to mature. A second might be that repetition is no bad thing. If the issues on debt were not clear after the last chapter, this one casts some more light on the issue.

◆

We have just had another week when the media has obsessed about what they call the UK's national debt. There has been wringing of hands. The handcart in which we will all go to hell has been oiled. And none of

1 https://twitter.com/RichardJMurphy/status/1366665012882857984

this is necessary. So this is a thread on what you really need to know.

First, once upon a time there was such a thing as the national debt. That started in 1694. And it ended in 1971. During that period either directly or indirectly the value of the pound was linked to the value of gold. And since gold was in short supply, so could money be.

Then in 1971 President Nixon in the USA took the dollar off the gold standard, and after that there was no link at all between the value of the pound in the UK and anything physical at all. Notes, coins and, most importantly, bank balances all just became promises to pay.

A currency like ours that is just a promise to pay is called a fiat currency. That means that nothing gives it value, except someone's promise. And the only promise we really trust is the government's.

If you don't believe that it's the government's promise to pay that gives money its value, just recall when Northern Rock failed in 2007. There was the first run on a bank in the UK for 160 years. But the moment the government said it would pay everyone that crisis was over.

There's a paradox here. We trust the government's promise, which implies it has lots of money, and we get paranoid about the national debt, which suggests the government has no money. Both of those things can't be right, unless there's something pretty odd about the government.

And of course there is something really odd about the government when it comes to money. And that is that the government both creates our currency by making it the only legal tender in our country and also actually creates a lot of the money that we usein our economy.

How it makes notes and coin is easy to understand. They're minted, or printed, and it's illegal for anyone else to do that. But notes and coin are only a very small part of the money supply - a few percent at most. The rest of the money that we use is made up of bank balances.

The government also makes a significant part of our electronic money now. The commercial banks make the rest, but only with the permission of the government, so in fact the government is really responsible for all our money supply.

This electronic money is all made the same way. A person asks for a loan from a bank. The bank agrees to grant it. They put the loan balance in two accounts. The borrower can spend what's been put in their current account. They agree to repay the balance on the loan account.

That is literally how all money is made. One lender, the bank. One borrower, the customer. And two promises to pay. The bank promises to make payment to whomsoever the customer instructs. The customer promises to repay the loan. And those promises make new money, out of thin air.

If you have ever wondered what the magic money tree is, I have just explained it. It is quite literally the ability of a bank and their customer to make this new money out of thin air by simply making mutual promises to pay.

The problem with the magic money tree is that creating money is so simple that we find it really hard to understand. We can have as much money as there are good promises to pay to be made. It's as basic as that. The magic money tree really exists, and thrives on promises.

But there's a problem. Bankers, economists and politicians would really rather that you did not know that money isn't scarce. After all, if you knew money is created out of thin air, and costlessly, why would you be willing to pay for it?

What is more, if you knew that it was your promise to pay that was at least as important as the bank's in this money creation process then wouldn't you, once more, be rather annoyed at the song and dance they make about ever letting you get your hands on the stuff?

The biggest reason why money is so hard to understand is that it has not paid 'the money people' to tell you just how money works. They have made good money out of you believing that money is scarce so that you have to pay top dollar for it. So they keep you in the dark.

There are two more things to know about money before going back to the national debt. The first is that just as loans create money, so does repaying loans destroy money. Once the promise to pay is fulfilled then the money has gone. Literally, it disappears. The ledger is clean.

People find this hard because they confuse money with notes and coin. That's not a good comparison. In a very real sense they're not money. They're just a reusable record of money, like recyclable IOUs. They can clear one debt, and then they can be used to record, or repay a new one.

The fact is that unless someone's owed something then a note or coin is worthless. They only get value when used to clear the debt we owe someone. And the person who gets the note or coin only accepts them because they can use them to clear a debt to someone else.

So even notes and coin money are all about debt. They're only of value if they clear a debt. And we know that. When a new note comes out we want to get rid of the old type because they no longer clear debt: they're worthless. When the ability to pay debt's gone, so has the value.

So debt repayment cancels money. And all commercial bank created money is of this sort, because every bank, rather annoyingly, demands repayment of the loans that it makes. Except one, that is. And that exception is the Bank of England.

So what is special about the Bank of England? Let's ignore its ancient history from when it began in 1694, for now.

Instead you need to be aware that it's been wholly owned by the UK government since 1946. So, to be blunt, it's just a part of the government.

Please remember this and ignore the game the government and The Bank of England have played since 1998. They have claimed the Bank of England is 'independent'. I won't use unparliamentary language to describe this myth. So let's just stick to that word 'myth' to describe this.

To put it another way, the government and the Bank of England are about as independent of each other as Tesco plc, which is the Tesco parent company, and Tesco Stores Limited, which actually runs the supermarkets that use that name. In other words, they're not independent at all.

And this matters, because what it means is that the government owns its own bank. And what is more, it's that bank which prints all banknotes, and declares them legal tender. But even more important is something called the Exchequer and Audit Departments Act of 1866.

This Act might sound obscure, but under its terms the Bank of England has, by law, to make any payment the government instructs it to do. In other words, the government isn't like us. We ask for bank loans but the government can tell its own bank to create one, whenever it wants.

And this is really important. Whenever the government wants to spend it can. Unlike all the rest of us it doesn't have to check whether there is money in the bank first. It knows that legally its own Bank of England must pay when told to do so. It cannot refuse. The law says so.

As ever, politicians, economists and others like to claim that this is not the case. They pretend that the government is like us and has to raise tax (which is its income) or borrow before it can spend. But that's not the case because the government has its own bank.

It's the fact that the government has its own bank that creates the national currency that proves that it is nothing like a household, and that all the stories that it is constrained by its ability to tax and borrow are simply untrue. The government is nothing like a household.

In fact, the government is the opposite of a household. A household has to get hold of money from income or borrowing before it can spend. But the gov't doesn't. Because it creates the money we use there would be no money for it to tax or borrow unless it made that money first.

So, to be able to tax the government has to spend the money that will be used to pay the tax into existence, or no one would have the means to pay their tax if it was only payable in government created money, as is the case.

That means the government literally can't tax before it spends. It has to spend first. Which is why that Act of 1866 exists. The government knows spending always comes before tax, so it had to make it illegal for the Bank of England to ever refuse its demand that payment be made.

So why tax? At one time it was to get gold back. Kings didn't want to give it away forever. But since gold is no longer the issue the explanation is different. Now the main reason to tax is to control inflation which would increase if the government kept spending without limit.

There is another reason to tax. That is that if people have to pay a large part of their incomes in tax using the currency the government creates then they have little choice but use that currency for all their dealings. That gives the government effective control of the economy.

Tax also does something else. By reducing what we can spend it restricts the size of the private sector economy to guarantee that the resources that we need for the collective good that the public sector delivers are available. Tax makes space for things like education.

And there is one other reason for tax. Because the government promises to accept its own money back in payment of tax - which overall is the biggest single bill most of us have - money has value.

It's that promise to accept its own money back as tax payment that makes the government's promise to pay within an economy rock solid. No one can deliver a better promise to pay than that in the UK. So we use government created money.

So, what has all this got to do with the national debt? Well, quite a lot, to be candid. I have not taken you on a wild goose chase to avoid the issue of the national debt. I've tried to explain government made money so that you can understand the national debt.

What I hope I have shown so far is that the government has to spend to create the money that we need to keep the economy going, which it does every day, day in and day out through its spending on the NHS, education, benefits, pensions, defence and so on.

And then it has to tax to bring that money that it's created back under its control to manage inflation and the economy, and to give money its value. But, by definition it can't tax all the money it creates back. If it did then there would be no money left in the economy.

So, as a matter of fact a government like that of the UK that has its own currency and central bank has to run a deficit. It's the only way it can keep the money supply going. Which is why almost all governments do run deficits in the modern era.

And please don't quote Germany to me as an exception to this because it, of course, has not got its own currency. It uses the euro, and the eurozone as a whole runs a deficit, meaning that the rule still holds.

So deficits are not something to worry about, unless that is you really do not want the UK to have the money supply that keeps the economy going, and I suspect you'd rather we did have government money instead of some dodgy alternative.

But what of the debt, which is basically the cumulative total of the deficits that the government runs? That debt has been growing since 1694, almost continuously, and pretty dramatically so over the last decade or so, when it has more than doubled. Is that an issue?

The answer is that it is not. This debt is just money that the government has created that it has decided not to tax back because it is still of use in the economy. That is all that the national debt is.

Think of the national debt this way: it's just the future taxable income of the government that it has decided not to claim, as yet. But it could, whenever it wants.

That's one of the weird things about this supposed national debt. When we're in debt we can't suddenly decide that we will cancel the debt by simply reclaiming the money that makes it up for our own use. But the government can do just that, whenever it wants.

This gives the clue as to another weird thing about this supposed national debt. It really isn't debt at all. Yes, you read that right. The national debt isn't debt at all.

That's because, as is apparent from the description I have given, the so-called national debt is just made up of money that the government has spent into the economy of our country that it has, for its own good reasons, decided to not to tax back as yet.

So, the national debt is just government created money. That is all it is. But the truth is that the people of this country did not, back in 1694 when interest rates were much higher than they are now, like holding this government created money on which no interest was paid.

You have to remember something else about those who held this government created money in times of old (though not much has changed now). They were the rich. If you don't believe me go and read Jane Austen's 'Pride and Prejudice' and note how much Bingley had in 4% government bonds.

And there was something about the rich, then and now. They get the ear of government. And so their protests about ending up with government money without interest being paid were heard. And so, money it might be, but from the outset the national debt had interest paid on it.

The so-called national debt still has interest paid on it. But then so do bank deposit accounts. And they look pretty much like money too. Only, they're not as secure (at least without a government guarantee in place) and so the government can pay less.

But let's be clear what this means. The national debt is money that represents the savings of those rich or fortunate enough to have such things on which interest is paid by the government because it's been persuaded to make that payment.

Let me also be clear about something else. Those savings are not in a very real sense voluntary. If the government decides to run a deficit - and that is what it does do - then someone else has to save. This is not by chance it is an absolute accounting fact.

Where money is concerned for every deficit someone has to be in surplus. To be geeky for a moment, this is an issue determined by what are called the sectoral balances. There's a government created chart on these here[2].

Chart 2.31: Sectoral net lending

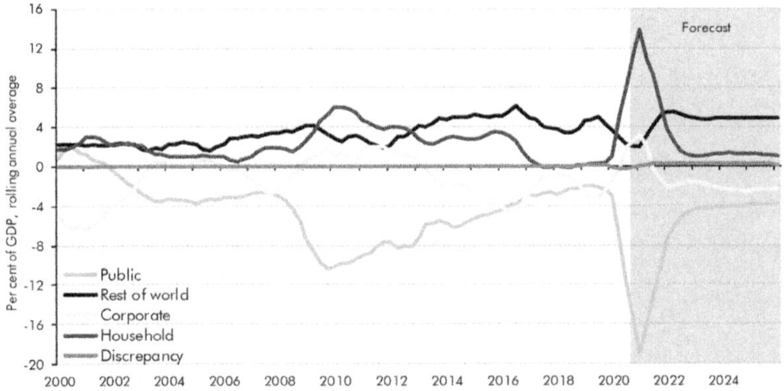

Source: ONS, OBR

The chart makes it clear that when the government runs a big deficit - as it did, for example, in 2009 - then someone simply has to save. They have no choice. And what they save is government created money. Which is exactly what is also happening now.

2 https://obr.uk/download/economic-and-fiscal-outlook-november-2020/ Since updated in March 2021

A growing deficit is always matched by savings. So who is saving? I am deliberately using approximate numbers, because they can quite literally change by the day. But let's start by noting that the most common figure for government debt was £2,100 billion in December 2020.

Of this sum, according to the government, £1,880 billion was government bonds, £207 billion was national savings accounts and the rest a hotch-potch of all sorts of offsetting numbers, like local authority borrowing. I don't think they do their sums right, but let's start there.

Except, these official figures are wrong. Why? Because at the end of December the Bank of England had used what is called the quantitative easing process to buy back about £800 billion of the government's debt, with that figure scheduled to rise still further in 2021.

I don't want to explain QE in detail here, because I have already done that in another thread[3].

So let's, taking QE into account, discuss what really makes up the national debt, starting with an acknowledgment that if the government owns around £800bn of its own bonds they cannot be part of the national debt because they are literally not owed to anyone.

Around £200 billion of the national debt is made up of National Savings & Investments accounts. That's things like Premium Bonds, and the style of really safe savings accounts older people tend to appreciate.

3 See earlier chapters

Around £400 billion of the national debt is owned by foreign governments, which is good news. They do that because they want to hold sterling - our currency. And that's because that helps them trade with the UK, which is massively to our advantage.

But what's also the case is that that because of QE UK banks and building societies have around £800bn on deposit account with the Bank of England right now. This is important though: this is the government provided money stops them failing in the event of a financial crisis.

And then there's very roughly £700 billion of other debt if the Office for National Statistics have got their numbers right (which I doubt: they overstate this). Whatever the right figure, this debt is owned by UK pension funds, life assurance companies and others who want really secure savings.

Why do pension funds and life assurance companies want government debt? Because it's always guaranteed to pay out. So it provides stability to back their promise to pay out to their customers, whether pensioners, or life assurance customers, or whoever.

So now I have explained how we get a national debt and that it's a choice to have one made by government. I've also explained that all it represents is the savings of people. And I've explained the government could claim it back whenever it wants. And I've covered QE.

So, the question is in that case, which bit of the national debt is so worrying? Do we not want people to save? Or, would we rather that they had riskier savings that put pensions at risk? Is that the reason why we want to repay the national debt?

Or do we want to stop foreign governments holding sterling to assist their trade, and ours?

Alternatively, do we want to take the government created money back out of the banking system when it's saved it from collapse twice now (2009 and 2020) and which provides it with the stability that it needs to prevent a banking crash?

Or is it the national debt paranoia really some weird dislike of Premium Bonds that suggests that they are going to bring the UK economy down?

The point is, once you understand the national debt it's really not threatening at all. And what you begin to wonder is why so many people obsess about it. To which question there are three possible answers.

The first is that the obsessive do not understand the national debt. The second is that they do understand it, but want to make sure you don't. And the third is that they realise that if you did understand the national debt there would be no reason for austerity.

Of these the last is by far the most likely. There's always been a conspiracy to not tell the truth about money, and how easily it's made. There's also a conspiracy to not tell the truth about the fact government spending has to come before taxation, and the law guarantees it.

And I strongly suggest that the hullabaloo about the national debt - which is a great thing that there is absolutely no need to repay and which is really cheap to run - is all a conspiracy too.

The truth is that the national debt is our money supply. It keeps the economy of our country going. It keeps our banks stable. And it also represents the safest form of savings, which people want to buy.

There is no debt crisis. Nor is the national debt a burden on our grandchildren. Instead, the lucky ones might inherit a part of it.

But some politicians do not want you to know that there is no real constraint on you having the government and the public services you want. What the government's ability to make money, sensibly used, proves is we do not need austerity. And we never did.

Instead, the opportunity we want is available. And we do not need the private sector to deliver it. The government can and should take part in that process as well, which it can do using the money it can create as the capital it needs to do so.

But in order to pursue their own private gains and profits some would rather that this is not known, so they promote the idea that money is in short supply and that the national debt is a danger. Neither is true. We need to leave those myths behind. Our future depends on doing so.

◆

7. The role of tax

The Covid crisis gave rise to widespread discussion of 'how are we going to pay for it?' That in turn led to calls for tax increases as 2021 began, which worried me enormously as the last thing a fragile economy needs is tax increases.

This thread[1] was written on 17 February 2021 in response to those calls and suggests a tax programme that would suit the needs of the UK post-Covid. Far too few people, including tax justice campaigners, are taking about this issue. This offering was intended to put that right.

That said, tax never excites people that much. This thread reached a bit over 90,000 people and had more than 5,000 reactions despite that. For tax, that's a lot.

◆

Tories are now saying there should be no tax rises this year. Overall, I agree. Right now we don't want overall tax increases taking demand out of a fragile economy. But that doesn't mean no tax increases. It means we need tax increases and tax cuts. Let me explain in a thread.

Tax is not all about raising revenue. Far from it, in fact. We now know that government can spend without taxing: the last year has proved that, for good. But that should mean that we also understand that tax has other important roles too, like tackling inequality.

1 https://twitter.com/RichardJMurphy/status/1361937728204636161

Inequality has always been significant in the UK. And Covid has made it worse. There has been a dramatic increase in unemployment. Many on furlough are on less than normal pay. And many self-employed people have been hit very hard. But others have seen their wealth increase.

We know why some have seen their wealth increase. When a government runs a deficit it's an accounting fact that someone else must run a surplus: the rules of double entry require this. This is, in fact, the only book balancing that is of importance when looking at government accounts.

And the government has run a deficit. It might be £400bn this year. To fund this (although the Bank of England denies it) the Bank's bought £290bn of government bonds between March and December 2020, pumping that much newly made electronic money into the economy as a result.

By chance the chief economist of the Bank of England has said that he thought savings had increased by at least £250bn during lockdown. There's a good chance he underestimated by £40bn, I'd say. The overall number will match the deficit and the QE that is funding it.

But that's an aggregate sum. In other words, that's the savings of all of us, added together. But that's not the whole picture. Because some in the country will have saved more than others. And as we also know significant numbers of people will now be borrowing to make ends meet.

Some of the borrowing cause by the Covid crisis will be new loans. Some will represent the running down of savings. Much will be informal. It will also be rent arrears, utility bills unpaid, and credit cards maxed out. The interest rate due on those borrowings is incalculable.

What that means is that the lucky ones have saved more than £290bn. Others are in much more debt to the same amount that some have saved in excess of £290bn. Because, again, that's what the accountancy of double entry always, ultimately, means. The Bank of England have underestimated savings by ignoring new borrowing.

Think about it. Overall, the best off will likely be at least £400bn richer this year, at least. And at the same time millions of people in this country will be suffering the anxiety of increased debt. And all because of Covid. Never, ever, presume that the world is fair. It isn't.

This is what the Tories want you to ignore when they say no tax increases now. And we shouldn't do that. We need increases in tax now because there is a massive, unearned, Covid gain in our economy that is creating inequality that is going to be corrosive in the long term.

Some of that gain is to be found in companies that have done well out of this crisis, just when other companies have been forced to the brink of oblivion. More is in speculative gains. Some of that will be in the City. And much of this will simply be increased personal savings.

So what do we do to tackle this? First, improve the position of the least well off. Increase universal credit, and not just by £20, which is clearly insufficient.

Then we also need to provide access to cheap loan funds for those in debt distress. It's the least the state can do. It can borrow for nothing, in effect. Why can't it share that benefit with those most in need, instead of saying them penalised by high rates?

And for those who think those idea of state backed loans for those who need them a very strange idea, maybe 80% of UK companies have such loans right now. Why shouldn't ordinary people get the same support when they need it?

After that, reduce taxes (and most especially national insurance) on the earnings of those on low pay, noting that income tax will make little difference for them right now.

There should also be council tax rebates for those on low pay, whilst in general the rates of council tax for the least well off who are likely to live in the lowest value houses should be cut.

Credits for utility bills could also be considered as support for those in need. They would be targeted and effective. People have a right to basic services.

Oh, and we should provide the BBC licence fee free to those on benefits, paid for by the government, and not the BBC.

Those are starters on what might be considered that could help those in need. But what about taxing to reduce inequality at the top of the income and wealth orders in the UK? This, I stress, is something we should do to tackle inequality though, and not because we need the money.

That point is worth repeating: we do not need to feel grateful to the rich for the tax that they pay. We now know that taxes are just part of the government fiscal cycle. Instead, we need to tax the rich more because they are rich.

And before anyone says this is the politics of envy, it isn't. This is about pure, hard-nosed economics. Being rich is problematic because the rich earn money from being rich. And most of that money earned from being rich is paid by those who aren't well off.

If you're in doubt that the least well off subsidise the rich, just call the payments from those with least to the who have most interest charges and rent and you'll see exactly what I mean. The fact is that if the gap between rich and poor is too big we create an unequal society.

And we also end up with a poorer society. That's because the rich will control more and more of the income, as they do now. They, though, will save more and more of that income, and that's a real problem.

The problem with too much saving is easily explained. It arises because the more that is saved in a society the less is spent on generating income. And as a result it ends up poorer as a result. Savings don't generate income. They may redistribute them, but don't create them.

So, societies that have too big a wealth divide don't thrive. Too much saving is one reason. But the wealthy also don't take risks. So they aren't entrepreneurs and don't create new businesses. That's because they're really frightened of losing the wealth and status they've got.

So the simple fact is that tax has to correct for these trends, or failings, if we are to have a thriving, innovative, and wealthy society, which a country socially divided by inequality cannot deliver.

So what to tax more? First, the obvious ones. First, we need to increase corporation tax, which is the tax on company profits. This will only hit the companies that have done well from Covid, of course. Only they will have profits. The rate is 19% now. It could easily go to 25%.

Then there is capital gains tax. First, make the rate equal to income tax. It is equivalent to income, so why not tax it as such? Second, cut the second tax free annual allowance that this tax gives to the wealthy. Why should they get two allowances when the rest get one?

Next, there's investment income like rents, interest, dividends, income from trusts or whatever else. People who work for a living have to pay national insurance on their earnings but the wealthy don't, but still get all the benefits. So introduce an investment income surcharge.

This investment income surcharge would be at 15% on all investment income over £5,000 a year, but higher for those of pension age. You have to be very wealthy to earn more than £5,000 of investment income a year right now. This is just creating a level playing field.

And then what? Remove the national insurance cap. Why should those on higher rates of pay have a national insurance rate of 2% on those higher earnings when most people pay at 12%? That's just not fair. So that cap has to go.

And another tax with a cap has to be changed too. That's council tax. The top bands, which are capped so that few pay more than £3,000 a year should be replaced by a new tax based on a percentage of property value. It's easy to do: property valuation is really not hard these days.

And while we're talking rates, why does income tax stop at 45%? Wouldn't 50% be fairer on incomes over, say, £300,000?

One or two more ideas. First, stop the tax relief that lets the wealthy claim back more tax on their gifts to charity than basic rate taxpayers can. Why should the rich actually benefit from charity? And the same is true on pensions - why should the rich get more tax relief?

Add all this up and a wealth tax can, to be honest, wait. That will take several years to introduce when some of the above could be happening in April. No wonder the Tories like the talk of wealth taxes - it puts off extra tax for a long time when we need it now.

Just a couple more things. How much will all this raise? Not £290 billion, I can assure you, which is by how much the government has increased private wealth as a result of QE. So the wealthy will still be winning hands down from this crisis. I am really not being unfair.

But how much precisely? I can't tell you, because anyone who is honest knows it is almost impossible to predict tax yields exactly when making changes of these sort. But I stress again, these tax changes are not really all about raising money. They are about tackling inequality.

Increasing inequality is the pernicious, so far largely unseen, consequence of Covid, and its impact may well last longer and be massively detrimental to millions of people's lives, whilst unfairly enriching many others. But Covid should have taught us we do live in community.

If that's the case then we need tax increases now. But the money raised should not be used to supposedly 'pay for Covid', because QE has already done that and it does not need to be reversed. The money should be used for a positive programme of redistribution.

This is what social justice should look like now. And this is what tax should be doing to deliver that social justice, now. Tax's ability to do this is what I called The Joy of Tax in my book with that title in 2015. It's what we need to discover now.

◆

8. Inflation

I published this thread[1] on 14 March 2021. Partly as a result it has not had the readership of some of the others – reaching only just over 30,000 people.

The thread had a particular purpose – which was to tackle the idea that inflation is inevitable because of the impact of quantitative easing. I do not agree with that but making clear why is really important – hence the reason for writing this thread and so chapter.

There is, however, another key theme in this chapter, and that is about the key political economy question of who is policy really written for? Asking the question 'who benefits?' is always key to political economy. The inflation debate is an essential part of that discussion because the choices made on how to manage it have significant impact on income and especially wealth distribution in the UK. Given how distorted both are already this is a very big issue in political economy.

◆

Current debate about inflation isn't really about whether it's likely: it isn't. Instead it's about whose vision of the future is going to win. Is it going to be the right-wing demand for small government that the inflation fetishists promote, or the one we need? A thread…

1 https://twitter.com/RichardJMurphy/status/1371037026242473985

Remember that the inflation that we are talking about is that with regard to consumer prices, which is often related to wages. It does not relate to asset inflation on things like shares, or house prices, which can behave quite differently, as the last decade has shown.

Since the 1990s central banks have been given the target of keeping inflation low. 2% has been the goal. But in practice as this diagram shows[2], the trend was already strongly downward before central banks were given this goal. Achieving it was not a problem as a result.

Chart 2: Global Inflation

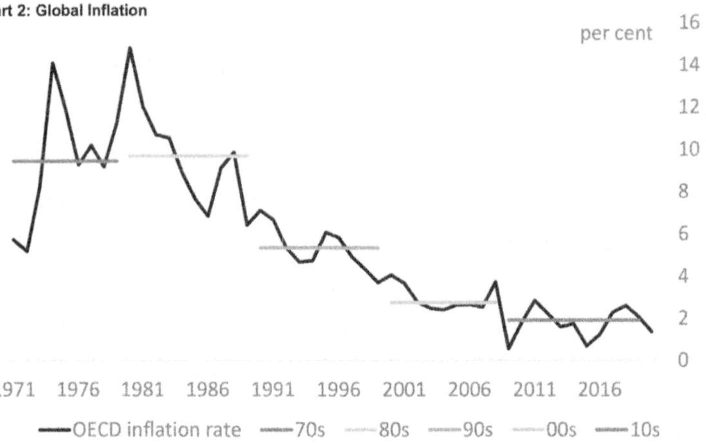

Source: OECD and Bank calculations.

It's also important to note interest rate trends[3]. These have been steadily downward over hundreds of years. There's no reason to think that central bank control of interest rates has had anything to do with this over the last couple of decades.

2 https://www.bankofengland.co.uk/speech/2021/february/andy-haldane-recorded-mini-speech-on-inflation-outlook

3 https://www.bankofengland.co.uk/working-paper/2020/eight-centuries-of-global-real-interest-rates-r-g-and-the-suprasecular-decline-1311-2018

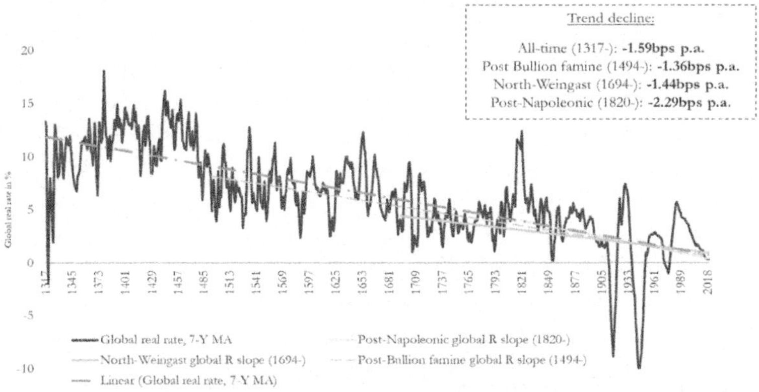

Figure IV: Headline global real rate, GDP-weighted, and trend declines, 1317-2018.

There are good reasons to think inflation and interest rates move in line with each other. If inflation is high interest rates need to be higher to pay real rates of return. The fact that the two move together is then unsurprising. But also reassuring, because they do.

It is also reassuring that the trend in the data is so persistent. The past does not predict the future, of course. But before I go any further in this thread it is important to say that the onus is on those who say this trend is going to be broken to say why that is the case.

I am not saying that inflation or interest rate rises are impossible in the future but I am suggesting that those who are suggesting that these are anything but very temporary phenomena have to explain why the trends of many decades are going to reverse now and for what reason.

Only two reasons are being given. One is that there is going to be excess demand after coronavirus. The other is that there will be a shortage of supply of goods and services in the economy to meet that demand. My argument in this thread is that neither is likely.

The first of these ideas says that if demand for a product rises and the supply does not then its price is going to increase. Economists would say this is so basic that no one could really argue with it. So let me do so.

First, this assumes that there are no alternative products available. The reality is that there usually are. Few things are so essential now that this is not the case. Secondly, this assumes we will not wait for what we want. We often will, and that smooths demand.

What is necessary then for inflation to happen is that not just one product must suffer excess demand, but that all must. Given that the diversity of products available usually makes supply shortages of this sort unlikely this has to imply something else is happening.

There are two options that can create this scenario. One is a general breakdown in supply. The other is a general increase in purchasing power. Of course, if they coincide that adds to the risk. That's the 'something else' those predicting inflation think is going to happen.

That something else that is happening is that it is assumed that wages, or spending power, or both are going to rise meaning there will be too much money pursuing too few goods, and so inflation follows. Any shortage in the supply of goods and services would exacerbate this.

Linked to this is the assumption that after the economy reopens there may be some supply disruptions. Part might be enforced e.g. an absence of foreign holidays. Some will be because businesses making what we want have failed. Others will arise because of slow restarts.

It may be easier to deal with this part of the issue than wages in the first instance. I would entirely agree that there will be supply disruptions after we get over coronavirus. It's impossible for it to be otherwise. Nothing works smoothly after such a massive close down.

But is it really plausible that we are going to suffer long term supply disruption after coronavirus? I think not. In fact, what the disruption has shown is just how resilient many of those parts of the economy supplying goods are, despite disruption.

And given government support much of the missing social economy will also bounce back very quickly, I suspect, when the opportunity is given. We may holiday at home and not abroad. We may even want to, to see friends again. But overall, we will be able to get what we want.

Brexit, of course, does not help in this scenario. But it is very largely a one-off shock. For inflation purposes the impact will probably be short lived and unlikely to last more than 12 months. Such things happen. But they are not indications of underlying inflation problems.

The assumption that we face long term supply constraints does not stack then. If either Brexit of coronavirus cause an inflation blip it will not last, and we need not worry about it in that case. So neither is the 'something else' that must be motivating inflation fears.

The 'something else' must, as a consequence relate to either a general increase in wages or a general increases in buying power in the economy not related to wages, but which might have the same effect of creating an overall increase in demand. Both options need to be considered.

Serious wage increases are incredibly unlikely at present. When nurses are offered a 1% pay rise and other public employees none at all because there is no private sector wage inflation anyone suggesting wages will be the cause of inflation is seriously misreading the evidence.

Anyone making that claim is also ignoring the state of UK unemployment. The government claims that this might reach a peak of in excess of 2 million people, but that claim is not a proper reflection of the truth.

Almost 5 million people are furloughed at present, and realistically some of them may not return to work when the crisis is over.

In addition, more than 2 million self-employed people are receiving support because their businesses have suffered as a result of coronavirus.

It's also been widely reported that millions of people have not qualified for employment help during this crisis. The precise number is, of course, not known.

Add all these up though and more than 10 million people are in vulnerable employment situations right now. Many of them will be looking for work when the opportunity arises once the coronavirus recovery gets underway. Many will be looking for the security of a regular wage again.

Put all those factors together and one in three people in the UK work force are highly likely to be looking for some change in their work, including a job change right now. And that makes serious wages increases very unlikely.

When there is a mass of willing and able labour looking for work - as is going to be the case in the UK over the coming years as people seek security after this crisis - the likelihood of wage inflation is very low.

To summarise then, supply issues that might push up inflation look to be pretty unlikely right now. And so too do wage increases that might push up inflation look very unlikely. So what else might create that inflation?

There is one other cause that I mentioned earlier in this thread. This is a general increase in buying power not related to wages, but which might have the same effect of creating an overall increase in demand. This is what the inflation fetishists are really worried about.

Despite the fact that supply is likely to meet most demand without disruption and despite the fact that wages are not going to increase much those obsessed by inflation think that demand is going to rise in the economy. And that is, they think, all down to government stimulus.

It is indisputable that the UK government has injected record amounts into the UK economy over the last year. Around £400 billion has been spent. More has also been made available by government backed loan schemes which are not a cost as yet.

It's also true that in some countries, like the USA, this stimulus continues. Biden is continuing to pump dollars into the economy in a way the UK government has now announced it wishes to stop doing by the autumn of this year.

The question is whether this stimulus will create buying power that might create general levels of price increase even though there are unlikely to be any major supply shortages. The answer is that this is incredibly unlikely, but why this is the case needs to be explained.

First, let's be clear that deficits were necessary. Without them vast numbers of people could not have stopped working. That was necessary to prevent the spread of coronavirus. Without that happening many more people would have died. The NHS would have failed, without a doubt.

Second, since more than 80% of the UK's businesses, and a higher promotion of employers, received government support it is fair to assume that a significant number of businesses would have failed during the lockdowns that were necessary to save life and the NHS but for this help.

Third, exceptional costs were incurred to tackle the crisis itself.

And fourth, whilst it's unpopular to say so, we still don't know that we have won this battle as yet. England might have a roadmap out of lockdown, but many countries are now going back into it. It is far from clear that this crisis is over as yet.

So, the spend was essential. And so too was the quantitative easing that funded it. I've already explained this in other chapters, so I won't do so again here.

I have also explained in previous chapters how the money that was required to fund these deficits was created, and so will not repeat that explanation again.

The point is, that what quantitative easing did was create new money. This is indisputable. That's what the Bank of England says it does[4]. That's not news then. Or a shock. It's a statement of fact.

But what is not a fact is that this leads to inflation, as some economists claim. They quote the quantity theory of money. This is a piece of economics that says if there is more money chasing the same quantity of goods prices go up. This is why they say we face inflation now.

They note that quantitative easing (QE) creates money without any more work being done and without any extra tax being due so they argue that this must lead to inflation. But they are wrong, for a number of reasons.

4 https://www.bankofengland.co.uk/monetary-policy/quantitative-easing

The most important reason is that they assume the government creates all money when making their claim. It is true that the government is important when money creation is being considered but it most certainly does not create all money. That's because banks also create money.

Banks create money by lending. That is how all money is created. So, when lending increases the money supply goes up. The corollary is that when loans are repaid then the money supply goes down. There are few other rules in economics as basic as that.

What happened in the last year are four things. First, people stopped borrowing. Consumers spent less (more than 20% less, on average) so of course their borrowing went down. The result was simple. The money supply was reduced as a result.

Second, people saved more. Given that the government protected many people's income that was inevitable if spending went down. And savings reduce the money supply. That's because loan repayment is saving in economic terms, and because savings take money out of the economy.

Third, government guaranteed lending to support business did not make good this shortfall. It kept business afloat, for sure, but the money created was not enough to tackle the money creation shortfall.

And, fourth, the government's own deficits massively

boosted savings. This is an issue I have already addressed in another thread, but it's worth repeating because this issue is so little understood.

When the government runs a deficit it, in effect, borrows. It's a simple accounting fact that someone must save as a result. This is explained in economics by something called the sectoral balances. This is the government chart of these in March this year:[5]

Chart 2.31: Sectoral net lending

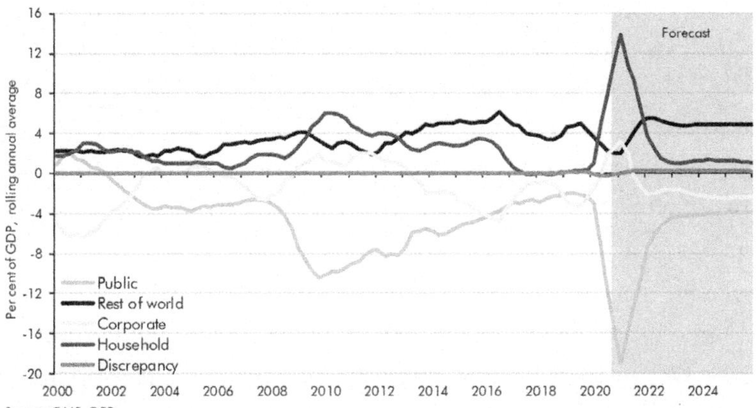

Source: ONS, OBR

The top and bottom halves of this chart are always equal. That savings equal borrowings is a fact. So, as is apparent, the government deficit has to create private savings. And it did. QE just added a twist. In effect the new money QE created went straight into private savings.

Now, not everyone was fortunate enough to see the benefit of that. In fact, many households are deeper in debt now than a year ago. Many more just got by. But the best off just got richer. That's what QE does.

5 https://obr.uk/download/economic-and-fiscal-outlook-march-2021/

This bias to the already wealthy within QE was not by chance. The Bank of England says that one of the aims of QE is to increase the value of financial assets[6], believing that this will increase spending. They achieved asset value increases. The spending increase I will get to.

For all the reasons noted, there's a glut of savings now. But that is because of the crisis. And it's because government created money has had to replace privately created in the economy. QE might have increased money supply, but the savings it's created has reduced it again.

In that case the claim that inflation is about to break out is hard to justify. So far the quantity theory of money is not a sufficient explanation for that. But, the inflation fetishists do not give up there. They still have another argument up their sleeve.

That argument is that this mountain of savings (much of which is held in money form) is all about to be spent. This is where, they say, inflation is going to come from without there being any increase in wages.

Andy Haldane, the chief economist at the Bank of England promotes this view. He thinks the economy is a 'coiled spring', waiting to burst. It will, he says, do so once Covid is over. Everyone, he thinks, is going on a spending spree of a scale never seen before.

The government and Office for Budget Responsibility also share this view. That chart on the sectoral balances reveals this. I share it again here.

6 https://www.bankofengland.co.uk/monetary-policy/quantitative-easing

Chart 2.31: Sectoral net lending

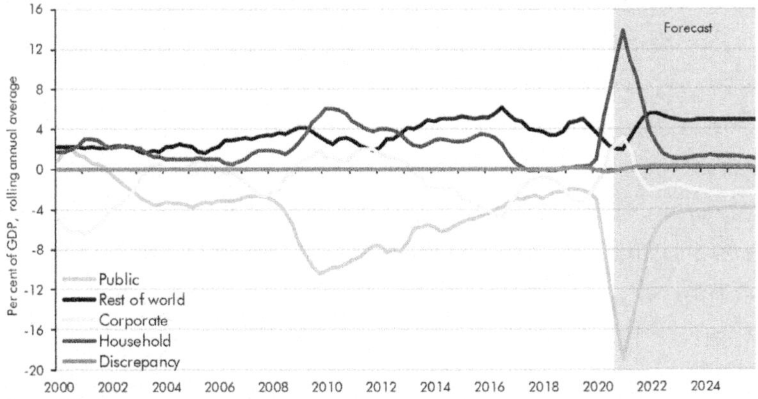

Source: ONS, OBR

The green line is overseas saving in the UK. The red line is the government's deficit. The yellow line is business saving / borrowing and the blue line the same thing for households. The bit that I am really interested in is the shaded section: the projections.

The government is forecasting that businesses already overburdened with debt because of Covid are going to borrow at near record amounts to fund investment and I can say with near certainty that they won't be, because banks will not be lending, and that ends that suggestion then.

The government projection for households is also wrong. By 2022 we are all supposedly going to have given up saving. But after 2008 it took until 2016 for this to happen, and the shock this time has been much more serious. There is simply no way this is going to happen.

The reality is that it is much more likely that after initial holidays, days out and meals out with friends that people are actually going to be pretty cautious. That's precisely because there has been, and is, so much uncertainty, and because people know wages aren't rising.

The exception may be amongst the very wealthy. They, after all, have more of the gains to spend than anyone else. So they might splurge a bit. They'll relate to the advertising mantra 'that they're worth it'. But there's something quite unusual that we also know about the wealthy.

The wealthy are wealthy precisely because they do not spend all of their savings. That's not rocket science, but it's also true. In other words, they will simply not spend enough to create the massive surge in spending the inflation fetishists think is going to happen.

The reality is now apparent. Supplies will be sufficient to meet what demand there is. Wages are not going to go up. People will save still because they are worried about their jobs. And the wealthy simply can't spend enough to create inflation.

I seriously doubt that anything much can create the persistent likelihood of inflation now. In that case one final question has to be asked, and that is will interest rates be increased? Around the world markets think that likely. But again I have to disagree.

Part of the reason why markets think interest rates will rise is because they think inflation will, and as I have noted these two are related. If I am right on inflation interest rates will not increase either.

Even if we do get a short-term increase in inflation e.g. because of Brexit, I do not see rates rising. The reality is that inflation has been well below target for a long time now. That means that the Bank of England can tolerate temporary upward blips without increasing rates.

There has to be a persistent threat for that increase to happen. And again, the lack of any real chance that business will borrow or households spend to the extent that the Office for Budget Responsibility suggests also suggests that there is no real threat of that happening.

In that case I cannot see any realistic chance of any significant increase in interest rates either. I could be wrong: all economic forecasting has to be caveated with the condition that 'it all depends on how events work out', but I just don't see it right now.

The reality is that the inflation fetishists are making their claims not because they believe in them but because they are living in fear of something quite different, and that is that the size of the state might grow after Covid.

The state is what the inflation fetishists really hate. And what they know is that society wants a bigger state right now. So they are using a false claim about inflation to try to prevent it happening. And they could win. As excuses go this is a winner, in their opinion.

But it's only a winner if we believe them, and there is no reason to do that. There are no real grounds to fear inflation. But there is every reason to believe that we need more spending on many aspects for what the state alone can supply.

The battle over inflation risk is not really about whether it's likely. It's about whose vision of the future is going to win. Is it going to be the right-wing demand for small government that the inflation fetishists promote or the one that we need? That's why this is important.

◆

9. The radio interview I want to hear

I posted this item on my blog[1] on 2 March 2021, the same day as the thread that is now chapter 6. As I say in it, I wrote in response to the frustration that no one seemed to be saying on the national media that the issues I address in this book, such as money, debt and tax, need not be viewed in the way that politicians seem to want us to think about them, and that they could instead be viewed very differently.

No politician has yet had the courage to follow my advice, but a BBC journalist, Andrew Verity, has been reflecting the opinions I explore in his reporting and commentary, and has confirmed to me that he has read at least some of the threads in this book. So, in some way my wish came true.

◆

I have been asked by some politicians to answer the question 'How we should we deal with the mountain of Covid debt?' which is the question that they all fear when facing a radio or television interviewer. This is my fantasy Radio 4 exchange:

1 https://www.taxresearch.org.uk/Blog/the-interview-i-want-to-hear-on-radio-4/

Interviewer: Let's face reality here. The country is more than £2 trillion in debt, and this has got to be repaid. What would you do about it?

Politician: I am sorry to say that I do not agree with the arguments implicit in your question, and I need to explain why.

First, the country has not got more than £2 trillion in debt. The government has bought back around £800 billion of its own debt. Quantitative easing has cancelled that debt. In eleven years not a single penny's worth of the repurchased debt has been sold back to the financial markets.

So, just like a paid off mortgage has been cancelled, so has this government debt been cancelled. In that case, I am not sure why you want me to explain how to repay government debt that has already been repaid? Your question doesn't make sense unless you're asking me how we would repay the debt twice, and I'm not sure why you would want us to do that.

Second, you say that government debt must be repaid, but the fact is that people are still queueing up to buy government debt. So, you need to explain to me why it is that the government wants to repay debt that people are desperate to buy? I am not sure I understand the reason for that.

Third, if you're asking how we could cancel the electronic money used to buy the debt, again, I am not sure why you would want to do that. The money in question – about £800 billion of it - is what provides our financial system with the stability it needs now. We could force that money of existence, but we'd destabilise the entire banking system if we did. Is that what you want, and why? Do you want another financial crisis?

Interviewer: But you know, everyone knows, that we cannot afford this debt. The Chancellor is already warning that if interest costs go up by 1% then the cost of government debt will increase by £25 billion. How can you not worry about that?

Politician: Again, your question really does not make a lot of sense, and I am going to have to explain why.

First, let's look at that £25 billion. Of that sum at least a third, and maybe a half by the end of this parliament, will be the interest that is still being paid on the government debts that the government has itself repurchased using quantitative easing, but which the government claims still exists to frighten us with numbers like this. So, I suggest half that £25bn of interest will come back to the government, straightaway. The real cost is just £13 billion in that case.

And of that £13billion part will be paid in tax. On average let's use 20% or so and say around £3 billion of tax will be paid. We're down to £10 billion now. Does that sound quite so painful? I thought not. If we get the numbers right they're nothing like what the Chancellor is suggesting.

Then remember that most government debt is fixed-term – and so on average it will take up to 14 years for some of it to see the interest rate change. In other words, this cost will not actually arise for a long time, if ever.

After which recall that interest rates are now almost entirely under government control because of QE. The old days when the markets ruled rates are long gone. So, the question is, why would the government want to increase rates? I wouldn't, so please don't ask me to justify the cost of something I would not do.

Interviewer: But come on, surely you agree that we cannot go on like this? There is no magic money tree. We can't just keep adding to the debt, can we?

Politician: Again, your question makes no sense, I am afraid. First, the national debt in the UK started in 1694. And as a matter of fact, it has increased almost without interruption since then. So, it would seem that 327 years of history says we can keep going on like this.

Second, there very obviously is a magic money tree: what we now know is that the Bank of England can create money on demand. That's always been true, but now we have seen it and can never pretend otherwise again. Why do you ask me to believe what is obviously not true in that case?

Third, we know Japan has created more than 200% of its GDP in QE and is still doing very nicely despite that. So, what the limit is in the case of the UK is not yet known, but it's likely we have a very long way to go.

Fourth, we now know the government can take almost complete control of interest rates in our economy. It's done so for more than a decade now. Real interest costs to the government have fallen as a result, and that's even before taking the impact of QE debt cancellation I've already referred to are taken into account
.

Fifth, because the government now knows it can use fiscal policy, monetary policy and QE to control inflation the risk of that is also very low now. Current paranoia is that we might reach the 2% inflation target after all, not that things are spinning out of control.

So, sixth, I can't see a reason why we can't go on like this.

Interviewer: You can say all that, but the Treasury, the Bank of England and the Office for Budget Responsibility all disagree with you. So why are you right, and they are wrong?

Politician: First of all, the IMF, World Bank and OECD would all say that the Treasury, Bank of England and Office for Budget Responsibility are wrong. I think you should ask why our public economists are arguing with the weight of world opinion, because that's what they're doing.

Second, the reason why they're wrong is that our public economists are still yearning for the old economics they were all taught back in their days at Oxford, or wherever. The nice mathematical models they learned that told them markets are always right and government is always wrong may have looked good on professor's blackboards, but that did not make them right.

Third, we know that those old economics models were wrong. A decade of austerity that left us wholly unprepared for the shock of Covid, and left millions impoverished and without the services they need, proved that. And the private sector did not deliver much growth. If anything, it just carried on destroying the planet whilst making this country more unequal.

Fourth, we know economics textbooks do have to be rewritten. The Bank of England itself said all the textbooks were wrong about money in 2014, when they admitted[2] banks not only could make money out of thin air, but that they did make all our money that way. But having done so, the Bank now refuses to take heed of its own advice and sticks to out of date dogma.

Fifth, there is politics in this. Tory governments want a small state. They will say whatever is required to deliver that, whether it is right or wrong.

Sixth, I think we need a bigger state than they suggest appropriate. That does not make me wrong. It means I have a different opinion, and one I think most people in this country would agree with.

Interviewer: So we're back to socialism then?

Politician: It's interesting that you think we've had

2 https://www.bankofengland.co.uk/quarterly-bulletin/2014/q1/money-creation-in-the-modern-economy

socialism because I don't recall that. Nor is it what I am calling for now.

I am arguing for a mixed economy where state and private sectors each do what they are best at. I think that dividing line is wrongly drawn right now. I think the state should do more and outsourcers should do less. The success of the truly NHS vaccination programme as opposed to the private sector track and trace programme is, I think evidence of that.

But that does not mean I am suggesting socialism. I want to build a partnership to create a transition to a full employment, sustainable economy. That is what we have to have. That is what is possible. But it is impossible if we try to crash the economy by repaying the national debt when it has already been paid, or by trying to crash the banks by withdrawing the funding that they rely upon. Recessions do not create investment and change, which is what we need. They create stagnation. And since private money is not creating that investment and change right now I am suggesting state money should instead.

So, a question for you. Do you want me to promote a recession or stagnation, as your questions imply, or sustainable growth and jobs, as I want? Is there even a choice to make? So why ask the questions that you do? Why not change the agenda to one that is appropriate for the times? Your listeners might thank you.

◆

10. Why does Boris Johnson want to take on the nurses?

This thread[1] was posted on 6 March 2021 when it became clear that the UK Budget was offering the NHS's nurses a pay rise of just 1% after a year in which they had been in what has become known as the 'frontline' of Covid care.

As I said in the introduction to this book, my approach to political economy is about problem solving. Theory is important, but dealing with real world issues is what I am interested in. This thread is an example of that. It reached 330,000 people, with over 27,000 interactions. Something about it must have worked.

◆

Why does Boris Johnson want to take on the nurses? Is this his union fight; a version of Thatcher's with the miners? Is the Battle of the Hospitals to be his Battle of Orgreave? And why? Thatcher wanted to break the unions. Does Johnson want to break the NHS? A thread...

1 https://twitter.com/RichardJMurphy/status/1368152593596354564

Even someone with the insensitivity of the average minister in this government must have realised that a 1% pay offer to the NHS would, after the last year, be treated as contemptuous, not just by the nurses themselves, but by many in the population at large as well.

We didn't clap for nothing. We have seen the exhausted faces. Few of us can really appreciate the trauma of going to work knowing we will see people die in greater numbers than we ever expected during that day. Nor can we imagine the feelings of helplessness that must induce.

I know the NHS is our religion. And there is this 'nurses are angels' thing. But some myths are based on facts. And I want to add in all the others as well, from the porters who make the NHS move, to the consultants, to the cleaners, GPs, and receptionists. They all make the NHS.

The last year's been about keeping the NHS open. Lockdowns saved lives. But they were really about keeping the number dying to a level the NHS could, just about, manage. All the sacrifice was to ensure that we could support those we lost, and those who helped them as they died.

Was that worth it? I think so. Few of us want to think about death. In our society it is a taboo. But Covid made us face it. Unexpected, early, unjust, heart-breaking deaths became commonplace, but not normal. And everything done was to give those dying the support they needed.

On the way, and due to incredible care, some brave decision making and simple determination it's also a fact that many who went to intensive care units also came out alive. Many, maybe most, are scarred. But they got another chance. And that's a cause for celebration.

The cost has been high. Hundreds of thousand of jobs lost. Countless cost to mental health. Failed businesses. Lives disorganised. Many hopes dashed. But, lives were saved. And, as far as was possible (and I know the constraints) those who died were respected, and cared for.

At the most fundamental level what is important within our society was questioned. And what mattered was one of last rites of passage: the preservation of life was enormously important, but so too was supporting those on their final journey. They had to die as well as possible.

I am not pretending that was always achieved. I know that it was not always possible. The care hone scandal showed that the government really did not understand this need at first. They should be held to account for that.

But if anything, this failure to protect some people, and the reaction to it, supports my narrative. We were angry about the indifference shown to those in care homes, and rightly so. Deep down, we still believe in the final rite of passage. Dying as well as we can matters to us.

It matters so much in fact that we were willing to throw our economy into chaos. We were willing to lockdown. We were willing to accept the consequences. The shock to

Dominic Cummings, very early on in this crisis, was that we cared about our grannies. He could hardly believe it.

There were those, Cummings and Johnson included at the outset, who believed Covid should be let rip. It should run through the population, do its worst, and leave behind the immune survivors. They eventually coalesced around something called the Great Barrington Declaration.

This was raw, market fundamentalist, survival of the fittest thinking. The natural winners should make it (no doubt motivated by a touch of eugenic thinking on who those winners might be). The rest were dispensable. More than that, they weren't worth the cost of saving.

Cummings and Johnson got this wrong. The cost of that was high. Their indifference to taking action early, because of their belief that simply letting the virus have its day was the right thing to do, has cost tens of thousands of people their lives in the UK.

But the fact was that in the end they knew people would not accept this. The indignity of letting people die in an NHS that was totally overwhelmed was something that they eventually realised would not be tolerated by people in the UK. We were willing to pay the price, and did.

I know that price has been very real. But, and I am back on economics now, in one regard there has been a shocking realisation. And that is that this price was not nearly as high as we were led to believe. Although we were told money was in short supply, it transpired it wasn't.

In the last year the government has had to spend around £400bn it did not have (the final cost is not known yet). And despite everything that had been said about taxpayer's money being in short supply, the money to settle the bills was available.

It was always going to be. There was never a doubt about that. And the government has always known the truth on this issue, even if there have been persistent lies about it. The reality is that the Bank of England has always been able to create money, on government demand.

This is simple to do. The government asks to borrow a billion from the Bank of England. The Bank agrees to lend it, which is pretty unsurprising given it's owned by the government, and simply records the loan in its books, and that's all it takes to create the money.

There is no printing press. No notes and coin are involved. Nor is any taxpayer. Least of all is any so-called 'taxpayer's money'. The government tells its own bank to lend it money, without ever agreeing a repayment date or interest rate, and it exists. Money, from thin air.

There always was a magic money tree. All the denials by all the politicians from all the parties who ever queued up to assure us that we had to 'live within our means' (which it transpired meant the money the commercial banks were willing to lend us) were talking nonsense.

We weren't constrained by the commercial banks. Or the money markets. Or the willingness of foreigners to lend to us. Nor did the government need to collect tax due before it spent. What a few of us knew, and most economists denied, was that the government creates its own money.

And it has. In the last year it's created more than £400 billion of new money. Costlessly. Without borrowing from anyone but itself. And it has injected that new money into the economy. It had to.

The Bank of England had to do this because private banks weren't creating new money, which is the only other way the money that keeps our economy going is made. And because many people were saving and paying down debt private bank created money was in short supply.

That's because saving and paying down debt takes money out of the economy. That's because all money is a promise to pay. So when a debt is repaid the money disappears. And when saving happen the money saved is not, by definition, spent and our incomes are other people's spending.

So, many people reacted to Covid in ways that were rational, but meant there was too little money in the economy. So, the government had to make good the shortfall, and it did, thankfully. And we don't need to worry about that.

Government created money is literally what makes the world go round. Once upon a time it was injected into the economy by increasing the national debt, but this time the demand was so big it was effectively spent directly. There is no real new debt as a result.

It's true that as a result of this money injection that the commercial banks now seem to have £400 or so billion more on deposit account with the Bank of England. But that means they are much less likely to go bust. That is a good thing.

And it's also true this new money does eventually end up as part of the savings of the already wealthy, because it pushes up asset prices (hence house price increases and a buoyant stock market despite Covid) and so taxes on the wealthy do need to increase to control that trend.

But is there any risk of inflation in normal prices as a result of this new money being created? I don't think so. There's a reason. It is that there are millions unemployed and underemployed in the UK right now. And that means there is no upward price pressure from wages.

So, back to nurses and their pay claims, where all this started. In my opinion the dispute to come on this issue is much more significant than the government has appreciated.

The government thinks there is no upward pressure in wages in the market right now. As a result their simple, dogmatic reaction is 'why do we have to pay in that case?' To summarise this thinking, it's that of the person who thinks markets always get things right.

But markets don't always get things right. The old adage that an accountant knows the price of everything and the value of nothing is based on a truth (and I am a chartered accountant). Markets can get values very wrong.

I think markets have got the value of nurses, and come to that, all in the NHS and care workers and all in education, very wrong right now. I'd go so far as to say that we are at a pivotal point in the development of society at this moment.

For forty years we have lived in what might be called the neoliberal era. The term is not as important as what it implies. And that belief is that markets know best. As importantly, the logic says that governments definitely know second best.

The power of this logic has been seen throughout our society, and in our politics. What we have developed are a breed of politicians who when they see a problem then think that whatever they, in government, might be able to do to solve it the market could do better.

So, they outsourced track and trace. They brought in consultants to manage Covid. And they believed that people with literally no experience in PPE could somehow deliver better product at lower price than experts on the issue, working in government.

They were wrong, of course. Track and trace and PPE are all disaster stories, to join so many other outsourcing catastrophes. The massive overpayments were just part of the story. The waste is another. Markets fail, badly, when managed in ignorance.

But, the government does not believe this. They swear these are success stories. And they regret the fact that limitations in the NHS - created by a decade of austerity from 2010 onwards - have forced them to close the economy down, all because people care about their grannies.

And, they think nurses are not in the market, so they know second best what their worth is. In that case they can be given what they get because only markets know the true price of anything, and value does not matter.

Except it does. Value is why we shut down the economy. We valued people: those struggling for life, and those losing it. Value is what shaped the last year. Value justifies what we did. And the government still does not get that, because they don't put a price on value.

And nurses are valuable. We have proven that. The worth is established. All that isn't is the price, which is something very different. And that conflict of market price versus value to society is the core of the dispute that I think is going to happen now.

The nurses are rightly going to ask to be valued. I think others should too. And they now know that the money to pay them is available. That's beyond dispute. What we face is a choice about the future of life in this country as we know it. All based on a 1% pay offer.

The decision to be made is about more than the nurses, important as they are. It is about who and what we value. Do we value essential public services? Or do we value the fripperies that some in society can afford because they pay less tax?

Do we value the claims of financial markets more than we value the right of government to decide how money is created for the benefit of us all?

Are we willing to tax the rich (who benefit by far the most from government deficits because the money injected into the economy ends up on their bank accounts at the end of the day) so we can have the services we need? Are we going to accept tough decisions for the sake of the common good, common values, common wellbeing?

This is the most massive question, and yet if the nurses pursue their pay claim - and I think that they should - then these are the questions that will actually be asked of us.

And surely we know the answers now? If everyone has enough to live on (and that's a massive 'if' we have not addressed as yet) then what we know now are a number of quite fundamental things.

The first is that we can't value a hug from a loved one. But we know how much we long for them.

And we can't estimate just how important friends are. But we do know we miss them, badly.

Dammit, we can't value a smile, and most of them are hidden now. Thank goodness they are reflected in our eyes, if we really mean them.

You get my point, I hope. There is no price for these things. But they are valuable.

As has as much dignity and care as possible for the dying been immensely valuable.

As was the sacrifice of those who had to deliver that dignity and care when no one else could.

The fight to come - for fight I think there will be - is about what is important. Is the claim that 'there is no money' (when there is) or that 'the debt must be repaid' (when none has been incurred, as the data shows) more important than caring?

I know the answer to that question. Deep down I suspect you do too. Deep down you might share my view of those who can't even understand that this is a question that needs answering, and who are willing to lie to deny it exists.

This, then, is a moment for political awakening. Not party politics, I stress. I don't much bother with them. But the real politics that determines the overall direction of our society.

From 1945 to 1979 the UK worked to recover and rebuild from war. From 1980 to date we have let markets decide how we live and have deferred our interest to the interests of those who pursue money, wealth and profit as if these matter most. And now? What are we to do?

I do not want to go back to 1945. We have learned too much. We have moved too far. That's not where we need to be. And anyway, that was a world that did not respect the equality that markets have not stopped us embracing of late. So this time is different.

But what do we want? That's to be answered. But the message that I am getting loud and clear now is that we want what is valuable, and that is something way beyond what markets deliver.

We want a straightforward, honest, clean, accountable state that will act openly and transparently in the public interest. We are a long way from that.

We want a state that is willing to invest in and protect our futures. That is not just about the NHS, of course. It is about free education. It is about cradle to grave care. It is about climate change and what we know must happen.

And it is about economic honesty. Economics has been used, quite deliberately, and I have to say with the willing consent of far too many economists, to bring us to the point where a government is apparently unable to value nurses.

Economics has deliberately created the myth that 'there is no money'.

And the economics that we have has been built on the idea that it is worth leaving people unemployed to keep inflation low, largely in the interests of preserving the wealth of the wealthiest.

This economics offends me. It is wrong, at every level. And there are alternatives that explain how the economy really works, starting from the core fact that the government can create all the money needed to create the society we want.

But we have to choose to do that. The nurse's pay claim is about making that choice. Precisely because it is I expect the government to oppose it, vigorously. And then they will say that if they must pay then the NHS must be privatised. I am sure that will follow.

This then is about the very essence of what our society is about. Are we to put value above price? People before profit? Society over private wealth? Community over markets? The smile of a friend over the heartlessness of the financier?

I know my answer. I know this pay fight, and the fight for the NHS that will follow, might be pivotal. This is about the very core of what it is to live in society. That is what I want. You need to do so too if we are to recognise what is of value in the future.

This is an issue in which everyone will have to take a side. But there can only be one winner if we are to have any chance of a decent future.

◆

Printed in Great Britain
by Amazon

10379225R00088